MW00632644

Five Hidden Mistakes
CEOs Make

How to Unlock the Secrets That Drive Growth and Profitability

By
Tom Northup

Published by Solutions Press

Five Hidden Mistakes CEOs Make
How to Unlock the Secrets That Drive Growth and Profitability

Published by Solutions Press
4533 MacArthur Blvd., #200
Newport Beach, CA 92660

c 2008 Tom Northup
All rights reserved

First edition printed May 2008

All rights reserved. Except as permitted by applicable copyright laws, no part of this book may by reproduced, duplicated, sold or distributed in any form or by any means, either mechanical, by photocopy, electronic, or by computer, or stored in a database or retrieval system, without the express written permission of the publisher, except for brief quotations by reviewers.

ISBN: 978-0-9752671-5-8

Printed in the United States of America

This is a work of non-fiction. The ideas presented are those of the author alone. All references to possible income to be gained from the techniques discussed in this book relate to specific past examples and are not necessarily representative of any future results specific individuals may achieve.

Five Hidden Mistakes CEOs Make
How to Unlock the Secrets That Drive Growth and Profitability

Contents

Foreword

This book is the summation of many years of first hand experience and research. It is written for CEOs, owners and senior managers. Throughout the book I use CEO as a shortcut to a wider audience. All of you are "CEOs" in your area of responsibility.

Successful CEOs understand that knowledge is key. They are always gaining knowledge that helps them manage and lead their companies. This book will provide that knowledge.

Executives of small to medium sized companies will find this book particularly compelling. Most of their experience is based in their functional area. They have no formal training in management and leadership. As their companies grow, they move past their comfort zones and find it increasingly difficult to successfully lead their companies to the next level.

They understand that for their companies to continue growing, they must do more than maintain the status quo. They must adopt a strategic mindset, transform their business, and change the way they operate.

All successful leaders want to achieve success for their companies. They want to grow profits and revenues year-to-year, beat the competition, and be pro-active rather than reactive in the marketplace . . . and they want to do it now.

To realize their future vision, successful leaders know they must strategically transform their companies, from leadership ability and people productivity to planning processes and even the underlying culture.

My objective is to help the reader develop the personal and organizational tools needed to dramatically improve performance and sustain it year after year... to not make just directional changes but to transform the company.

The book presents a management system that accomplishes this objective. I develop the system by discussing five hidden mistakes executives make that kill sustainable growth. To build excellence at all levels, executives must minimize or eliminate the effects of these mistakes.

This book provides practical tips that you can use immediately to improve your business. A lot of what you read here will validate what you already know. That's good. We need to be exposed to concepts several times before we become comfortable with new knowledge. Take the opportunity to refresh your thinking and learn different effective methods of reaching success.

Knowing something and doing it are two different things. 80% of success is taking action. My goal is to help you get the maximum possible advantage from reading this book; to get you to think about how you can take effective personal and organizational action.

Each chapter starts with a quotation to get you thinking. You will find yourself remembering them because of their simplicity. At the end of each chapter I will present what I believe to be the best ideas in the chapter. In the blank space below my ideas, you can write your best ideas as they relate to your specific circumstances. With each *Best Idea* I suggest you also write a measurable goal to build improvement into your organization.

Review your notes to maximize your retention. We retain 80% of what we see, hear, write, and review. Discuss and teach key employees this material and your plan for incorporating it into your company. Work to retain the information that is important and relevant for you.

You may be interested in my qualifications. I spent my first career in manufacturing management. In my last three companies, I was the CEO and a principal. In one situation I led the company to over 600%

growth in five years, taking the company from an industry also-ran and positioning it as a world leader in its field.

I now work with CEOs to help them reach sustainable revenues and profitability, establish competitive advantage in their marketplace and build an effective management team. Appendix One, About the Author, gives more information.

Lastly I acknowledge the many people who have assisted me in writing this book. I quickly understood my limitations as a writer. This book would not have been possible without the expertise and gentle prodding of my editor, Lee Pound. Lee has the ability to edit style and presentation without changing content.

I would like to acknowledge the contribution of three key alliances. Leadership Management Institute, LMI, of Waco, Texas. LMI for over 40 years has been a pioneer in leadership and organizational development. Its programs are written in 20 languages and used in 60 countries. Participants in the LMI process make permanent behavioral changes leading to more successful lives. LMI has been instrumental in developing my thinking in productivity, development, leadership and generating results.

Patrick Below of Madison, Wisconsin has spent his career in strategic planning and his insights have shaped my thinking in this important area. Mike Weaver, Bucks County, Pennsylvania, and I have had in-depth discussions about strategic development that have developed my expertise in how to effectively build an outstanding organization.

I am deeply indebted to my associates around the country who have contributed valuable insights and expertise: Ray Stuchly, Riverside, Illinois; John Dame, Harrisburg, Pennsylvania; and Rich Lewine, Montgomeryville, Pennsylvania to name a few. Of course I couldn't have completed this with out the backing and understanding of my wife Katie.

1
Competitive Imperative

**"If we do what we've always done,
we will NOT get what we've always gotten."
Mike Weaver**

Do you control your company or does it control you? What do you think about when you plan your day?

Do you focus on *problems* such as whether your managers are accomplishing all you would like, whether you are meeting your sales and financial expectations, or whether obstacles seem monumental?

Do you focus on *opportunities* such as how you will produce new orders on time, how quickly you can expand your bank credit line to handle new opportunities, or how quickly you can expand the sales team to exploit new products?

The difference between these two approaches is the difference between a weak organization not meeting its performance objectives and an outstanding organization that is a profitable, growing market leader. Organizations have battled with this difference throughout history. Recently the difficulty of dealing with this condition has been greatly magnified by the lack of time we have available to bring about change.

Just 20 or 30 years ago we could operate successfully under the "Christopher Columbus" school of management.

1. When he left, he didn't know where he was going.
2. When he got there, he didn't know where he was.
3. When he got back, he couldn't tell where he had been.

However, he got there and back three times in seven years. Which means Columbus was operationally very competent.... even though he never knew where he was!

Columbus had the luxury of time. Seven years. Today we don't have that luxury and time can become our enemy. A few years ago the business cycle was much longer than it is today. The ever changing pace of technology, a greatly shrinking competitive world and the instantaneous transfer of information make managing a company today much more challenging than it was for our parents.

The telephone is my favorite example. In the 1950's the phone used a dial and was black. Over several years, it evolved to add push buttons and one color, beige. Now phone features change every few months.

These changes were directional. Transformational changes are now emerging that will redirect the phone industry in ways we couldn't imagine only a few years ago. Cell phones are challenging the status quo. Our children use their cell phone as their primary personal phone. How many households will have a standard phone in a few years?

Hurricane Katrina ushered in more far-reaching change. The storm put standard phone equipment under water and blew down cell phone towers. The first phone communications in New Orleans in the aftermath came over the Internet. Internet communication has the opportunity to completely change how we communicate.

We are all familiar with this saying: "If you do the same thing over and over, you will get the same result." Given our rapidly changing world, technology and information availability, it is more appropriate to say: "If we keep doing what we have always done we will NOT get what we have always gotten."

Small to medium sized companies are particularly vulnerable. We are all aware of industries that have been greatly impacted by change. Many of us are living through these changes right now.

Companies with proprietary product lines are vulnerable. Flower pots, once primarily made in the United States, now mainly come from Asia. Large pots weigh 30 pounds or more. We might think the bulk and weight of pots would insulate domestic manufacturers. Not true. Asian pots are landed in the United States for much less than the cost of domestic production.

Companies in traditional sub-contractor industries, precision metal forming for example, are also affected by foreign competition.

Foreign competition is attacking the top line of the Profit and Loss statement, the basic revenue these companies generate. The very existence of the company is in jeopardy. These companies are unable to lead their markets and must compete through value innovation. Their leaders have experience in their functional area. They understand how to make incremental changes but have no experience in coping with the transformational changes being forced on them.

These extreme examples show how competitive situations cause change. Whatever situation drives change, we need continual awareness of what is happening in our industry. Our market is quickly forcing change on us. Since change will continue, we will be more effective when we proactively react to it.

Knowledge is the key. Without it we cannot go to the next level. Once we gain the knowledge, we must use it. My favorite comment is, "No great manager, no great leader ever fell from heaven. It is a learned skill, not inherited." To be successful we need to learn to use the knowledge we have.

In 1937 Andrew Carnegie, the Bill Gates or Warren Buffet of his time, commissioned Napoleon Hill to interview 500 of the most successful people in the world. Carnegie wanted to find out if successful people had common characteristics. He opened doors for Napoleon Hill to talk to industrialists, presidents, great inventors like Henry Ford and Thomas Edison and even Gandhi.

The result was the book *Think and Grow Rich* written by Napoleon Hill and published in 1937.

Hill found that successful people developed mastermind alliances. They didn't manage alone, they built teams. They utilized specialists in areas where they didn't have expertise.

In many situations where the outcome is vital to our business, we discover that we don't have the necessary expertise. By establishing relationships with others, we create an effective way to achieve the results and success we desire.

Another way to gain knowledge is to use the experience of others, such as an advisor who supports you and shows you how to proceed. This advisor won't let you make repeated mistakes and will hold you accountable. This is alliance building at its best. An expert who has been there and done it can assist you to develop outstanding performance when it's really important.

Some alliances are easy to understand. We use alliances with our CPAs and attorneys to ensure compliance with basic business and legal requirements.

Other alliances are less easy to envision but can have a dramatic impact on our performance. They include:

Sales: Companies often reach a plateau when the sales department grows to the point where employees and processes would benefit from experience not available in house. Often CEOs who lack a sales background become frustrated with the lack of results. Even though top line performance is critical to business success, many CEOs are reluctant to seek expert advice.

Hiring: We all say people are our most important asset yet we fail to hire the right people.

Executives of small and medium sized companies often have limited experience in evaluating and hiring people. Many executives don't have the cash flow to hire professionals so they conduct the hiring process themselves without expert assistance.

The hiring process is an opportunity to improve the capability of your staff. Studies demonstrate that matching a candidate's skills and personality to the job requirements has a major effect on performance and turnover. Yet many don't take the time or have the patience to hire effectively.

Personal interviews provide limited information to the untrained questioner. Assessments offer an inexpensive and accurate first step. They provide facts about the candidate that seldom surface in an interview such as learning ability, personality characteristics, motivation and fit with organizational culture and values. Even knowing this, many companies refuse to spend the few dollars assessments cost.

People Development: Most companies have maintenance budgets; IT for example. How many have a budget to develop their most important asset, people? Personnel development is specifically designed to improve effectiveness by changing behaviors and attitudes. A small improvement in the effectiveness of key people has a great impact on the bottom line.

Strategic Planning: Organizations with a specific plan significantly out-perform other companies of equal capability. Very few CEOs know how to conduct a planning session. Successful CEOs hire outside facilitators to maximize the benefits of strategic planning. Skilled facilitators bring out the best from all participants. As neutral parties, they overcome the political and hierarchical environment. They use proven systems, ensuring that the company's plan is a product of the team's best input.

Our competitive environment puts pressure on organizational performance, people and leadership. Personal leadership is extraordinarily important. Working harder isn't effective. We have to work smarter. Working hard just means putting more and more time into the effort. But what if you're not doing it right in the first place? Going faster and harder is not going to get you where you want to go.

We have to be smarter about how we do things. We need to develop excellence in all areas of our company. We need to minimize, even eliminate, the five hidden mistakes and develop sustainable revenue and profitability.

The Five Mistakes: A Case Study

The five hidden mistakes are not difficult to understand. They represent blocking and tackling for management. We all make them to some extent. Effective CEOs know they can always be better. They seek knowledge and then put it to use to build an outstanding company. For instance, a top sports team may be number one but they still practice the basics every day.

The five mistakes are lack of focus, development, practice, planning and accountability. An excellent company has a clear strategy and effective operations. Success in overcoming the five mistakes brings sustainable growth in revenue and profitability, competitive advantage and market innovation.

A case study demonstrates how overcoming the five mistakes generates outstanding achievement and continuing success.

This is an example of how an American manufacturing company, using centuries-old technology, survived in the global marketplace. Through the development of a comprehensive strategic plan, the establishment and execution of specific, measurable goals and improving the effectiveness of management, the company survived a dire time in its history.

Case Study

Situation

For more than 80 years Kopp Glass was the industry leader in molded, blown, and precision glass for technical, industrial, and commercial applications. Their products are used every day, all over the world. The company's success begins with the unique glass science they have spent years defining. Their optical engineering expertise and ability to meet strict quality and tolerance requirements defined their many years of success.

September 11, 2001 had a sudden and detrimental impact on the company. They lost a significant portion of their business due to the rapid decline in airline industry sales. Over the next two years, the company found itself in a downward spiral with an unrecoverable loss of revenue. The company's direction was out of focus. With a successful 80-year track record to boast about, the employees never imagined their company being in this seemingly irreversible state.

Solution

Bob, the CEO, was determined to pull the company out of the tailspin. In April of 2003, he and the executive team embarked on a program to regain financial stability through cost reduction, increased productivity, increased sales and higher profit margins.

He knew that in order to recover some of the loss in revenue, the company had to develop and implement a solid plan. The management team developed a strategic plan that determined the company's position in the marketplace, identified it's customers' key success factors and identified how to make these core competencies of Kopp. They created a production goal that would bring an increase in the average revenue generated per hour in production by 40%. They developed a number of sales, production, and quality initiatives directed at improving this key productivity measurement.

Bob understood that weak operating performance was a function of leadership. He implemented a management development program to improve performance. Bob and his executive team focused on changing production practices and eliminating products that were not contributing to the standard.

Outcome

Within months the company was operating at a break-even level. Less than 12 months later, the company's sales had increased 18%. Combined with increased productivity, the company generated its first profit in three years. In the second year sales were up an additional 28% and profit had recovered to historical levels. By 2005, they reached their production goal and overall productivity had grown by 28%. Through the efforts of a strong leader and a dedicated staff, the downward spiral was halted.

What did Bob and his team do? They overcame the five hidden mistakes. They focused their talents, developed individually and as a team, practiced, planned and executed.

Whether you address the pain of missed expectations in current operating results or look to exploit growth opportunities, overcoming the five hidden mistakes will bring you success. Of these, future success is much more enjoyable. Get in the habit of waking up thinking about opportunity, success and continuous growth in revenue and profitability.

The balance of this book takes us through the knowledge we need to lead our companies to competitive advantage, sustained growth and profitability that meet our expectations, and to proactively lead the change that the world, technology and information transfer impose on us.

Chapter 1 Best Ideas

Develop an attitude that we are always searching for knowledge to more effectively manage and lead.

Develop mastermind alliances to build organizational excellence.

My Best Ideas and Goals to Meet Them

_____

_____

_____

_____

_____

_____

_____

2
First Mistake: Lack of Clarity and Focus

"There is nothing more wasteful than becoming highly efficient at doing the wrong thing."
Peter Drucker

Relentless global competition and rapid technological advances make managing and leading a company more challenging than ever before. Successful CEOs know they must align their organization to proactively react to their environment. They understand their top challenges as:

- Creating a culture that embraces and adapts to change
- Stimulating employees' innovation and creativity
- Getting the whole company to understand and execute strategy.

An effective CEO understands that he cannot meet these challenges if the management team does not work together. He knows that he can meet them when he and his management team focus on working on the business.

Focus is one of the most important management skills a CEO can develop. Focus is intentionally directed and magnified attention. Focus drives performance, performance drives results. Having a focused management team is the key to developing competitive advantage in your marketplace. Focus means getting everyone on the same page and the right page so that everyone works together.

Lack of focus is a fundamental mistake many executives make. Focus has an impact both tactically and strategically. In this chapter we will explore focus from a tactical perspective. In Chapter 9 we will delve into the strategic implications.

Efficiency vs. Effectiveness

We often confuse efficiency and effectiveness even though they are very different concepts. How would you define efficient? How would you define effective? Before continuing, take a moment to consider your responses.

Efficiency commonly means getting a job done quickly, on budget and without loss.

Effectiveness means performing activities that help us go to new levels and doing them in order of priority.

Efficiency is *doing things right*. Effectiveness is *doing the right things.*

Which do you believe is more important? Which will produce the greatest results, efficiency or effectiveness?

Of course we want both. However, the correct answer is effectiveness. When you spend time doing things right, but not the right things, you will not get the results you expect!

Many managers make the common mistake of being efficient but not being particularly effective. Every day "crisis managers" act in an "efficient" manner by always working on tasks that are urgent or seen to be urgent. They allow no time to manage and communicate and never enough time to adequately plan or monitor the plans they make.

Just like Christopher Columbus, they are operationally very competent. However they fail to create results that are important to the organization's growth and future success.

An effective manager focuses on important tasks that drive results and success, tasks that are important to the future. Nothing dramatic will happen if he doesn't attend to them; he just won't progress to the next level.

High Payoff Activities

We are most effective when we work on our High Payoff Activities (HPA): those activities that generate the most success for our company at our level of responsibility. High payoff activities are usually not urgent. They do not act on us; we have to act on them. It's the 80/20 principle. The more time we spend on our HPA the more effective and successful we become.

HPA are the proactive ways to increase success, yet how many of us know what our HPA are? How many of us have given them concentrated thought and written them out? Once we identify our HPA, how many of us set measurable goals to accomplish them?

From a team perspective, how many of us help our key people determine what their HPA are? Have we assisted them to set goals to meet their HPA?

An effective CEO generates strong focus for the company when he holds in-depth discussions, sets goals and determines accountability. Manager's HPA support each other and the team works together towards a coordinated result.

Examples of High Payoff Activities

The most important of our HPA is to regularly plan and organize our time by placing those activities most important to our success into our daily routine. When we schedule important activities and conflicts arise, as they always do, we can make a conscious decision about which one needs our immediate attention. Importantly, since we are aware of the tradeoff, we reschedule the activity that we have delayed. In this manner we keep our success activities on track as we continually reevaluate our routine.

The benefit can be personal. If we are having difficulty working on our success activities, we realize that we may need to change the way we conduct our work day. This becomes a personal HPA.

Many executives have functional responsibilities which, after planning, are often the most important HPA.

Examples: People Development

Larry Bossidy, former CEO of Allied Signal, provides an example in his book, *Execution: The Discipline of Getting Things Done.* He tells us that he spends over 20% of his time on people development. This CEO of a billion-dollar company with extensive demands on his time understands that people development is a key HPA necessary for the future success of his company.

Another example comes from Paul, owner of a service company. Paul and his company had reached a plateau. Paul is the primary salesperson in the company but he was spending less than one day a week in sales. He was hands on in the rest of the business thinking there was no other way to get the work done right. After all, he started the company and knew the best way to do every job. As a result he was struggling to maintain sales volume.

Paul determined his HPA was to spend more time in sales. He set a goal to spend 60% of his time, three days a week, in the field in front of prospects. He focused his activities to achieve his goals. Over time he improved his time spent in sales to over 60%. His company is now growing at a rapid pace and he is opening a satellite office.

Paul's need to spend more time in the field was an obvious HPA. Not so obvious was Paul's management style. Paul needed to delegate effectively to his staff. This entailed building trust in his staff so that they could independently manage their responsibilities. This was the personal HPA Paul needed for his success.

Beyond performing these functional responsibilities, effective managers must work on the organization rather than in the organization. True HPA for the senior executive are activities that develop and stimulate employees through coaching and mentoring, build a culture where people want to do their best, monitor results, and develop personal leadership.

The effective leader understands that working on the organization is not natural. He creates HPA to continually modify his attitudes about work. You can do the same by asking thought-provoking questions that will guide your thinking towards your HPA. These questions include:

What can I do to:

- Provide the people with whom I work clear performance objectives?
- Create a culture in which people feel included and valued?
- Be a better leader?
- Create systems to make work more error free?
- Increase the value our customers receive?

A complete list is included in Appendix Two.

Executing HPA

If we don't know our HPA and schedule them, daily activities will take precedence and we will not be as successful as we would like. Having clear and measurable goals is an important component if we are to execute our HPA.

Contrast two companies. The first is poor at identifying, developing and executing organizational goals. In the second, each employee focuses on completing three to five goals that are aligned with other departments and management. Which organization do you think will come out ahead?

Effective CEOs focus themselves and their people through the goal setting process. They limit the number of organizational goals to only a few that are key to success and can be given full attention by staff – four to six is normal. Too many or too few will diffuse focus in the organization.

It is important for goals to be consistent between functional departments. This brings win-win scenarios. If there is conflict between Marketing or Sales or Production, the organization will work at cross purposes with less than optimal results. It is equally important that employee goals be consistent with organizational goals from first level supervision through top management.

Goals should be balanced between financial and non-financial areas. A budget and financial goals do not go far enough. Non financial goals, such as developing outstanding customer service, are important to developing an excellent organization.

Goals should follow the SMART acronym: Specific, Measurable, Action oriented, Realistic and Tangible.

A study by Robert Rodgers of the University of Kentucky and John E. Hunter of Michigan State University, showed that goal setting, in combination with participation in decision making and objective feedback, yields average productivity gains of 56%.[1]

A system of goals is the most effective way to build efficiency and effectiveness. Goals enhance organizational and individual performance with no investment in infrastructure. Effective CEOs don't refuse a deal like this!

Example: Productivity

Bob Hand of Kopp Glass has had to increase the company productivity goal two more times from the original. "I never thought that we could reach such high productivity levels so quickly. A lot of credit goes to the goal setting method."

For effective goal setting, work on your goals regularly. Develop action steps, get them into your schedule, measure progress and hold yourself accountable. The secret of success is determined by our daily agenda. We can spend our time fixing our past or working on our future. Make your daily routine future oriented.

Multi-tasking - A Caveat

Industry and individuals have embraced all of the high tech trends and gadgets. We pride ourselves on our multi-tasking ability,

[1] Journal of Applied Psychology, 1991, Vol.76, No.2

often juggling blackberry, internet and phone connections almost simultaneously, performing several tasks at once rather than concentrating on one task at a time. By placing ourselves on call 24/7 we respond in real time and regularly interrupt ourselves.

We think our connectedness makes us faster and more efficient. In reality, as we flit from one task to another, we lose efficiency and more importantly we lose effectiveness. Recent research finds that people complete less work in a day than they did a decade ago and that the number of people who call themselves successful has dropped 30%.

This loss of personal productivity is harmful but not nearly as harmful as the loss of personal communication. The humorous cartoon in which techies rely on e-mail instead of walking down the hall for a personal conversation is a sad but true social commentary.

The high tech industry developed through some of the most creative teamwork and personal communication in history. It is ironic that today's executives use high tech as a way to avoid using effective personal communication.

In 1970 the newly formed Palo Alto Research Center, PARC, became a great example of how to put technology to practical use. According to Alan Kay, one of the wizards of PARC, the strategy for letting creativity flourish was to "get really great people together and manage the social dynamic." He added that, "No organization works beyond the size where you can get all the principals together in a room and thrash out the issues before you go home."

In 1979 PARC allowed Steve Jobs and his staff to look at their technology. Jobs immediately understood the potential and built a team of marketers and engineers to commercialize the technology. The Apple Macintosh story is now legend.

What did both PARC and the Mac teams have in common? They focused attention on their goal. They encouraged unfettered continuous communication. Both teams kept rules to a minimum. However, the one PARC rule that everyone had to obey without exception was that no one could miss the weekly meeting.

Not communicating face to face limits our effectiveness and our ability to drive results. When we are not face to face we miss tones, inflections and non-verbal communications. Without face to face interaction we cannot have in-depth give and take to fully expand our ideas.

High tech equipment and email have not fulfilled their promise to streamline work. Multi-tasking has actually reduced success. We regularly interrupt ourselves and as a result lose focus and the ability to complete tasks in a timely manner.

Summary

Most people stress becoming more efficient. Efficiency is important, but if we are to reach higher levels of success, we need to work on those activities that are vital to our future. Although these activities are not urgent, we must act on them. We have to identify them and place them on our schedule.

Knowing which duties are high payoff activities is important to developing personal focus. A best idea for the CEO is to work with his management team to help them define their HPA. This is an effective way to get the team focused and on the same page.

If we want a future that is different from our present and want to accomplish this in a proactive and timely manner, we must meet the challenges of technology and competition head on.

Focus drives performance, performance drives results. Effective CEOs understand that creating focus in themselves and their management team is the key to success. Focus is fundamental to developing competitive advantage in our marketplace. Focus on those activities that drive success.

Chapter 2 Best Ideas

High Payoff Activities drive effectiveness.

Focus drives performance, performance drives success.

Focus is fundamental to competitive advantage.

My Best Ideas and Goals to Meet Them

_____

_____

_____

_____

_____

_____

3
Share Power to Increase Effectiveness

**"You do not lead by hitting people over the head –
that's assault, not leadership."
Dwight Eisenhower**

Focus in our management team brings competitive advantage. Using High Payoff Activities, we can get everyone on the same page. However, how do we get everyone on the right page?

We get everyone on the right page and develop focus and management effectiveness when we share power with our management team. Sharing power is one of the most effective traits a CEO can develop.

Time and geography are no longer barriers to change. Today market forces bring continuous change. We are able to react proactively when we share power with our management team to ensure they are not change inhibitors but change agents.

23

World War II and the Korean conflict were instrumental in establishing the leadership techniques in vogue for the past several decades. Since the 1950's a common management style has been the command and control model. Traditionally managers using this style are assertive, decisive and controlling. They take risks and make changes with a high energy level while demanding that others work to their expectations. They get results so they are highly sought after as managers.

The flip side is they are difficult to work for. As a result, the controlling leader struggles, employees refuse to make an emotional commitment, the management team does not work in a unified fashion and the organization suffers.

In recent years, management experts such as Jim Collins in his book *Good to Great* have shown that a more effective way to develop excellence is to share power with key people in the organization.

Even the military is changing. In the book *It's Your Ship*, the author, Captain Mike Abrashoff, discusses how he was traditionally trained by the Navy as a command and control officer. When he took command of a ship he found it difficult to meet the combat readiness, reenlistment and other objectives of naval command. He sensed the need for a more effective management style and changed his command and control leadership style to one of sharing power through employee empowerment.

We have become more knowledge based. Successful change is driven by knowledge. Sharing power in the management team leads to shared knowledge. Shared knowledge leads to stronger performance. Performance drives results.

Companies get the results — good or bad — that they are designed to get. A management team that works together to proactively effect change becomes a major organizational strength. If your vision for the future differs from your current situation, if you want different results, then you must change the way you manage. If you don't, how can you expect results that differ from those you have already achieved?

Until a few decades ago most people worked for one or two organizations their entire career. Today workers move from job to job and career to career with little difficulty.

Younger employees have not experienced hard times and lean business cycles. They are used to highly charged environments where technology regularly challenges them to improve job performance. They expect to quickly gain responsibility and become part of the decision making process.

Organizations create excellence by hiring highly effective employees and giving them challenges. Good managers, to keep good employees in today's highly mobile job market, create an environment where management values employee expertise and rewards their contributions. Good people don't leave their positions for higher salary and benefits. They leave because they don't feel appreciated or effective in their position.

Four benefits of sharing power are instrumental to developing excellence in the organization and competitive advantage in the marketplace. The first two, more tactical in nature, bring immediate results. The second two, more strategic in nature, focus on longer term results.

Tactical Benefits of Sharing Power
1. Change Initiatives

In today's competitive environment management must react quickly to rapidly changing market conditions and incorporate transformational, not just directional, changes.

Change, though pervasive, is often misunderstood. Many myths affect our attitudes toward it and limit our ability to proactively accomplish positive change. Too often we react defensively to circumstances that appear beyond our control. Let's take a closer look at five myths about change.

Myth 1 — Change must be imposed. People don't like change. We must coerce them to make changes.

Real change is self motivated. It's not that we do not like change. What we do not like is to be changed. When we don't involve our employees in discovering the need for change and don't involve them in the change plan, they become "change plan critics."

We all know of situations where a manager announces a change he wants to incorporate into company processes. After six months he's disillusioned that the staff has not implemented the change. Usually, it has died from inertia on the part of change-resistant staff.

Managers who participate in setting direction or developing initiatives become intellectually and emotionally committed. When management is part of the solution, it doesn't resist change, it welcomes it. Change becomes part of the fabric of the company.

Example: Sharing Power

Fred, the owner of his company, decided the company could improve service by centralizing customer service. He gave the directive. His managers resisted, giving many reasons why this was a bad decision. Fred delayed implementation and brought his managers together over several meetings to discuss why and how to improve customer service. With discussion the management team agreed that centralizing customer service would provide great benefit to the company. Fred was responsible for implementation. When the project fell behind schedule, the managers pushed Fred to speed the improvements!

An effective leader understands that sharing power is the most effective way to build personal motivation. Employees must take intellectual and emotional ownership of change initiatives. They must understand how their job relates to the vision of the company. When they are part of the change process, they develop personal commitment to the outcome.

Myth 2 — *You gradually wear down resisters. Eventually everyone will embrace change.*

As we learned in Myth 1, you can work with the people who openly resist your plans. They will slowly respond to your leadership.

However, you cannot ignore those who do not openly protest. These problem employees, the "amen brother" types, appear to accept changes. In reality the more changes you incorporate, the more these silent resisters sabotage them in subtle ways.

While they may openly play your game, they are working for the status quo. They think that they can, "wait this out for a while, and soon everything will be back to normal."

It is not necessary to change all employees at the same time. Concentrate your initial change efforts on the management and key people in your company to get them intellectually and emotionally committed. After that your combined team effort will build trust and commitment in all employees.

Myth 3 — *Change is a one-time thing. Once we make the changes we need, everything will be OK.*

The world changes continuously and companies must change with it. If you suspect that change will be difficult, plan for it. After all, the time to repair your roof is when the sun is shining.

Effective leaders build a culture that embraces regular change through the use of continual planning. A culture that emphasizes planning develops management agreement, personal commitment and team focus. With these conditions present, you proactively lead change with the support of your team.

Myth 4 — *Change is radical.*

Real change happens in small steps. Large changes overwhelm people, defeating them before they start.

When we break the change initiative into small steps, people maintain enthusiasm because they see positive progress in short time periods. Prioritize these steps so the results lead to the success of the overall initiative.

Leaders that track and measure the success of each step of their initiatives most often accomplish their goals — and as the leader of your company, you must hold yourself accountable. When you take small steps, it is easier to redirect your effort as necessary. People responsible for change remain positive because they see the results of their efforts.

Myth 5 — *Others have to change, not me.*

Too often the attitude of the leader is "My people need to change, not me." In reality, the most effective change initiatives are proactively led by top management. You must lead change if you want your organization to change.

As an effective leader, you play a key role as a positive role model. People respond positively to shared initiatives and team effort. When top management is actively involved, you and the company are better able to respond to the inevitable twists and turns that arise.

These five myths impact our ability to make necessary and effective changes in time frames that allow us to proactively impact our marketplace. Accept these myths as fact and you are likely to fail. Debunk these myths by acting proactively and your chances of success increase exponentially.

Share power by involving managers in the planning process; develop personal commitment and team effort to build agreement and focus; break change initiatives into manageable pieces; be proactive; hold yourself accountable; know that tracked and measured plans get accomplished — this is the credo of the successful leader.

2. Organizational Culture

Effective employees of all ages want challenges. Workplace studies that evaluate job satisfaction consistently identify the top three areas of importance as:

1. Corporate culture
2. Opportunity to use skills and abilities
3. Opportunity to learn and be creative

Example: Management Style

Captain Abrashoff's results were dramatic. After changing his management style equipment failures dropped 68% resulting in a 25% savings in the ship's maintenance budget. The ship's readiness indicators soared over 60%. Most importantly, the ship's reenlistment rate improved to well over the navy's average and in two critical categories went from 28 to 100%.

The area most commonly thought to be in the top three, financial reward, was number nine on the list.

How does this relate to us? How many of us would like to spend less on maintenance and other overhead costs? How many of us are satisfied with our employee turnover rates? Would we prefer to reduce our employee replacement costs?

The way people perceive their company has a significant effect on their performance. Daniel Goleman's work on emotional intelligence clearly identifies the advantages of working with and through people. His research says that an effective organizational culture can have up to a 25% positive effect on performance. By sharing power, the effective CEO cultivates a results-based culture of enthusiastic, motivated, and confident employees committed to achieving their organization's future vision.

Allow Employees to Add Value for Competitive Advantage

The most important way we use power sharing occurs when we empower employees to add value to the organization. Give your employees permission to add value as they do their jobs. Trust them to do their jobs with great competence. Give them the authority to make decisions that benefit the company, benefit customers and generate revenue.

For example, allow customer service representatives the freedom to solve customer complaints in ways that best serve the customer, even if it means they need to make an exception to company policy. Give sales representatives the authority to establish price with customers. Allow employees the opportunity to serve the customer in ways that build sales, loyalty and growth.

An appropriate question is: Don't we lose control when we allow employees to make these decisions? We often think they are not capable of making such decisions.

When we centralize policy with management we set a ceiling on the margins we will attain. At this level, management effort is centered on ensuring we meet budget.

As expected, when we empower employees but give them no guidelines, we will create lower margins. For example, the salesman will take the path of least resistance and always give the lowest price.

For empowerment to be effective we must train our employees and give them proper incentives, knowledge that will allow them to make informed decisions and training to understand how their contribution brings value. Incentives are important. For example, tie sales incentives to the margins their sales contribute, not to sales volume.

The benefits of empowering employees are dramatic. Involve your employees in developing change initiatives and give them the opportunity to add value. Empowered employees build a positive culture where they assist each other. They want to do their best. They will help you accomplish amazing results.

Strategic Benefits of Sharing Power
1. Planning
The single most important activity a CEO can undertake is to develop and implement a strategic plan. An effective leader understands that allowing his team to contribute to determining the direction the organization will take leads to highly effective planning. Good planning raises the team's effectiveness to a level that can't be reached by any other means and creates a very strong team working with mutual trust and shared accountability. Planning is discussed in detail in Chapter 9.

2. Best Thinking
Wise leaders know that sharing power generates organizational best thinking far above that which one person can accomplish alone. They draw on the combined wealth of knowledge that employees, with their differing professional interests, experiences and perspectives, bring to their jobs. Best thinking is discussed in detail in Chapter 10.

Summary
Sharing power is an effective method of getting everyone on the right page, creating positive change and molding a culture where people want to work.

Successful leaders have many of the traditional traits we value. They differ in one key area. They use their power and demonstrate their competitiveness through working with and through people. They exhibit social awareness through developing others, understanding their organization, being a change catalyst and building cooperation and teamwork.

Successful CEOs understand that one of their most important high payoff activities is to build a culture where sharing knowledge becomes routine. Managers encourage their teams to think more strategically and build best thinking into the organization every day. Change is a constant in the positive culture of the company.

By staying in control, you weather the difficult periods. By being proactive, you build a "let's beat our best" change philosophy into the culture of your organization.

Shared power is the catalyst that:

- Raises the effectiveness of an organization to a high and sustainable level.
- Develops individual and team focus tactically and strategically.
- Builds personal motivation among team members.
- Encourages members to become change agents, not change critics.

The result of sharing power is organizational excellence. The company builds a competitive advantage in the marketplace by being proactive and leading rather than by being reactive and following.

Remember positive change brings positive results. Real change should be vastly satisfying . . . and fun!

Chapter 3 Best Ideas

Sharing power with your team is a very effective management trait.

Build change into the culture of your company.

Allow employees to build value for outstanding results.

My Best Ideas and Goals to Meet Them

_____

_____

_____

_____

_____

_____

_____

4
Second Mistake: Lack of Development – Economic Reason

**"The biggest room in any organization
is the room for improvement."
Anon**

The paramount challenge for a CEO is to improve revenue and profits. Successful CEOs do this year after year because they understand that people implement improvements. In this chapter we discuss the economic justification for people development. In the next chapter we discuss the strategic justification.

Successful CEOs focus their attention on the development of key staff members who make the greatest impact. They understand the economic imperative of people development: that a small improvement in the effectiveness of their people brings about a much greater impact on profitability. People development generates organizational excellence. Continuous people development is a competitive advantage.

Every organization has two things in common: a present and a future. Everything in between is process. Process is important; the quality of the processes we use determines our results. If you want a different future you must change processes.

People lead change. For positive change you must have individual and organizational growth. We need to become more effective if we are to steadily improve our results.

Most people think of personal growth as training. A more comprehensive definition of personal growth is development. There is a big difference.

Training is reactive, such as learning a new software application or gaining knowledge in schools.

Development is specifically designed to change behaviors and attitudes, which is the way we act and think. Development is results based. We specify a process improvement and get predetermined results.

To tie into our discussion of focus in Chapter 2, the key lesson is: training improves efficiency, development improves effectiveness.

Economic Justification of Development

What is the main difference between companies in your industry? Your product or service is similar. Your procedures and processes are similar. Almost always, the reason some companies struggle while others grow and prosper is the skill and ability the management team possesses. Often the single largest overhead expense is the combined salary of the management team.

"People are our most important asset" is an overused cliché. Yet how many of us truly understand the point it expresses? If they are a key asset and a large expense, what are you doing to improve their effectiveness? Our key people drive the processes that determine our future success. To achieve stronger results we must continually develop their effectiveness. As they become more effective, they are able to significantly impact the bottom line.

Figures one and two give the economic justification for development. Every organization employs key staff to manage production of their product or service, sales and overhead. The first chart shows representative costs for these functions. Costs lead to profit, in this case 6% of revenue.

Key staff employed to	Cost
Produce	33% of Revenue
Sell	15% of Revenue
Control	15% of Revenue
Profit	6% of Revenue

Figure One

If key staff members achieve a 10% performance improvement, we will generate a much larger increase in profit.

A 10% improvement in the effectiveness of key staff reduces cost.

	Cost	Reduction
Produce	33.0%	3.3%
Sell	15.0%	1.5%
Control	15.0%	1.5%
		6.3% reduction

Original Profit	6.0%		
New Profit	6.0%	plus	6.3% = 12.3%

Figure Two

The 10% improvement has a profit impact of 205%.

Of course every organization is different. The basic understanding: a small improvement in the effectiveness of key personnel always has a much greater impact on profitability.

What employee level constitutes key staff? The answer is: all managers in a position of responsibility. First level supervisors have the most direct influence on employees. Their decisions affect profitability every day. When they are new in their position and inexperienced, developing their people skills, effective planning and accountability will bring immediate benefits that will quickly transfer to the bottom line.

More senior managers regularly make decisions that have long term effects and can impact the company's direction, revenue and profitability. Small changes in the development of these managers have a major effect on profitability and competitiveness.

Successful CEOs understand the economic value of development and its relationship to profit. They do not consider development a cost but an investment similar to investments in technology, equipment or process.

A CEO's challenge with any investment is to realize the projected ROI. When they invest in buildings, equipment or processes, CEOs have control. The project's momentum builds until it permeates the organization. As momentum builds, the CEO may reduce his direct involvement.

Realizing an ROI in people development is different. People control themselves and have differing needs. Changing personal behaviors and the attitudes that drive development takes much time and effort. In this environment, the CEO must maintain continuous leadership. Employees will not continue their efforts to make changes if the CEO is not actively involved in the progress.

Another example from Larry Bossidy illustrates this. He says that there is a gap between what a company's leaders want to achieve and the ability of their organization to achieve it. Bossidy understood that excellence of execution requires a comprehensive understanding of a business, its people and its environment.

Example: Development

> Bossidy returned to Allied when the company was in decline. He immediately worked to improve the effectiveness of his people. For the first two years he devoted between 30 to 40 percent of his day to developing leaders. He understood the effort and commitment required. The payoff was greatly improved performance and results.

In most organizations the largest overhead cost is the combined salary of management from first level supervisors to the CEO. We budget for improvements in technology and process. Yet how many of us budget for improving the effectiveness of ourselves and our key people? I don't mean just improving skills; I mean developing effectiveness to manage and lead.

The practical answer is that besides the basic lack of understanding of the relationship between development and results, we are unwilling to spend the emotional energy and personal time to effect people change. Continuous people development becomes a personal high payoff activity for the CEO who wishes to make a dramatic change in his organization.

The commitment for continuous people development from the CEO is critical. This commitment starts with him. One CEO of a sales organization eloquently voiced his passion and commitment.

Example: Commitment

"We have a terrific team of dedicated individuals who I truly believe want to be LEADERS within our organization.

None of us have really had much "formal" training. We are all trying to manage through intuition, common sense, etc... and while it has worked in many ways... the complexities of our business require a different approach!

We have all embarked on a road together... to enhance our management skills!

Is it challenging... you bet!

Is it time consuming... you bet!

Is it extremely difficult to balance our day jobs and still stay on track... you bet!

Are we going to stay the course... you bet!

Where are we headed...

It's not about developing new forms.....

It's not about doing homework assignments.....

It's not short-term....quick fix... then back to our past....

We need to evolve as leaders!

We need to communicate effectively!

We need to work together to be the management team that makes a difference!

I've made the commitment to support this

> process...
>   I need each of you to remain committed to being the best you can be!"

Small improvements in the effectiveness of management bring much larger changes in the bottom line. In one year sales in this $100 million company increased 18% and net income increased almost $4 million.

A Caveat

One critique we often hear about people development is, "We develop our people, they change jobs and we don't get the benefit."

Good people have career options. In fact, good people don't leave a job to get higher salary and benefits. They leave because they don't feel appreciated or effective.

Good people want challenges. They enjoy working in an environment where management seeks their expertise and values their contributions. The effective CEO shares power by encouraging his key staff to help develop initiatives and set direction. People who are part of the solution become intellectually and emotionally committed to the organization.

Good people expect to meet their personal goals as they help the organization meet its goals. An effective CEO recognizes that people follow a leader because of what the leader can do for them. He understands his staff's individual motivators and works to help them achieve personal success.

Summary

A CEO's challenge is to continually build revenue and profit. To accomplish this year after year, successful CEOs change the processes that drive their business.

People lead change. There is a definite relationship between organizational growth and personal development.

Successful CEOs understand that personal development is an investment where they can expect a positive ROI. They understand that their personal involvement and leadership is required to ensure the positive return on their investment in people.

Successful CEOs understand that a small improvement in the personal effectiveness of key people has a much greater impact on the bottom line.

The unavoidable conclusion: personnel development is a catalyst bringing competitive advantage into your marketplace.

Chapter 4 Best Ideas

Development of people makes economic sense and provides competitive advantage.

My Best Ideas and Goals to Meet Them

_____

_____

_____

_____

_____

_____

_____

5
Second Mistake: Lack of Development – People Reason

**"The greatest thing about tomorrow is
I can be better than I am today."
Tiger Woods**

In Chapter 4 we discussed the economic justification for development. Small changes in effectiveness generate much larger changes in profitability. In this chapter we will discuss development as it relates to our employees.

The way people think about their company has a significant effect on their performance. There is a positive connection between the culture of the company and employee performance.

The effective CEO understands this. He builds a culture where people can perform to their high standards and reach their personal goals. As they reach their goals, the company has equally outstanding success.

All organizations are perfectly designed to achieve the results they are now getting. The culture of the organization is the framework that sets the tone for high performance.

Jay Hall, PhD., of Teleometrics, using data from over 100,000 managers, conducted landmark research to determine if he could find a difference between high, average or low managerial achievement. His research definitively shows that the common behavioral characteristics top achieving leaders employ sets them apart from their lesser achieving colleagues. He categorized managers into five categories and identifies the "Developer" as the highest achieving management style.

The Developer leader is the most effective managerial type. He assumes that most people actually like to work, seek meaningful, fulfilling and stimulating work, and want to do their best. He brings success through improving the talents of his employees. Developers use their power not for personal motives but to enhance the quality of work life for all employees.

The four other types are, briefly:

The Taskmaster views employees pessimistically, believing people work because they have to and that they lack self direction. He provides strong controls within the context of a very strong task orientation. He relishes personal power and uses negative reinforcement with employees. Hall determined that a Taskmaster is about half as effective as the Developer.

The Comforter is exceptional at giving support to employees and seems to not ask for much in return. Like a parent he protects employees, viewing them as dependents. He practices a good deal of rationalization. He may be a little more effective than the Regulator.

The Regulator is a low risk taker and will default to the "regulation." He feels he is powerless to make changes and will seek to avoid personal hassles. He too believes employees only work because they have to and he is powerless to do anything about it. He is only about one-fifth as effective as the Developer.

The Manipulator has subtle interpersonal abilities and may be versatile with employees. He views all people as easily finessed. He is primarily motivated by his own needs and is about as effective as the Taskmaster.

Developer CEOs build a culture where people want to be and want to do their best. All you have to do is to create a team of enthusiastic, motivated, confident, grateful, committed people working together - with a high degree of cooperation and esprit de corps - on behalf of a future vision they have all committed themselves to. Easy to say, difficult to do.

Personal development is the key to continuous organizational improvement and is one product of an effective culture. Thus building a performance culture becomes a key high payoff activity of Developer CEOs.

Many individuals strive to regularly improve their performance. If we improve our effectiveness by only 1% a month, we will double our effectiveness in about five years. The same holds true for organizations. If the management team can similarly improve its effectiveness, the organization's performance will improve as well.

CEO developers build a performance culture and assist their employees to continually improve their performance. The combination creates a competitive advantage in the marketplace.

Development Process

There are three important areas to consider: appreciation, who we work for and why employees follow a leader.

1. Appreciation

William James, called the Father of American Psychology, identified appreciation as one of the most basic human qualities. Observe your employees. You will notice that all of them have the letters MMFA emblazoned on their foreheads: "Make me feel appreciated."

Who wouldn't want to hear the following words from an employee?

"It's more than just a job to me. I REALLY like working here. The people I work for are great, all the people here are great and my boss takes care of me."

A good compensation plan is commonly thought to be an effective method to develop employee appreciation. A more thoughtful view is that compensation is actually a financial obligation of the organization to the person doing the job they were hired to do.

Financial incentives are particularly important for people seeking basic living and security needs. Financial incentives lose importance for well paid executives looking for esteem and self actualization needs.

The bonus component of the compensation plan is thought of as a financial incentive and as a way to demonstrate appreciation. In Chapter 6 we will discuss incentives like bonuses and see how temporary they can be. Today's incentive is tomorrow's expectation.

Financial compensation is one way to measure success. A good salary and regular bonus can create a satisfied employee. However, satisfied employees will still test the market for better opportunities with similar compensation levels.

The alternative is building loyalty in employees. There is a difference between satisfaction and loyalty. The loyal employee doesn't think about alternatives. He has a high threshold for even discussing alternatives. He just isn't interested.

Sincere appreciation for the person, the results he brings, his experience and his commitment develops loyalty. We give appreciation by choice to let people know they are valued.

A developer leader believes people want to do a good job and want to be appreciated. These leaders regularly acknowledge the achievements of their employees who help build a positive culture of performance.

2. Who We Work For

How many of your employees wake up in the morning, look in the mirror, smile and say, "I can't wait to go to work today?" How many of you have this attitude?

Follow that question with, "Who do your employees work for?" Who do you work for?

A sophisticated view is that you are paying your employees to work for themselves. In reality we all work for ourselves. When we understand this we go to the next revelation. Work can be a blessing, not drudgery.

How can the humdrum of the work day and demands of the job be a blessing?

We spend a lot of time and energy in our job. We have an idea of the personal success we want from a job. Reaching a sales level or being promoted through the organization are two examples. When we clearly know where we want to go then work allows us to structure our time for our benefit.

Of course all jobs have their repetitive and non-stimulating moments. However, when viewed as a blessing, work offers the opportunity to grow. When you clearly visualize the payoffs you will enjoy from success in your work, the activities of your profession cease to be meaningless. They become a labor of love, a game, a fascinating adventure. You reach for a higher plateau each day.

When you learn the joy of work, success comes not at the end of a battle, but as the culmination of a game. Each day is exciting. Every day you enjoy progressively larger and more intense rewards as you move toward the full realization of your long term goals.

Your most effective employees understand that they really work for themselves. You want to retain these employees because of their positive attitudes. Because they have a positive belief about work, they continually develop their capabilities.

3. Leadership Levels

John Maxwell, author of many books on leadership, identifies five levels of leadership relative to employees as:

1. Position – have to follow you
2. Permission – they want to follow you
3. Production – follow you out of respect for your results
4. People development – follow you for what you can do for them
5. Personhood – follow you because of who you are

Our position and title gives us authority and responsibility. To be effective we have to earn permission and respect from our employees. This is the basic reason unions were established in the Twenties; employees were unhappy with how management responded to their needs.

People will follow a leader when he has great experience. A simple example is a successful professional. Many young lawyers went to work for a Melvin Belli or Johnny Cochrane because of their outstanding record of achievement.

Personhood relates to extreme circumstances and the leader of the times. Two examples are Winston Churchill leading England during World War II and Lee Iacocca leading Chrysler out of its massive bankruptcy.

The key to leadership in a business is to understand that people follow us for what we can do for them.

Successful people want to feel appreciated, work for themselves, and follow a leader for what he can do for them. To be effective we need to have significance in the lives of our employees or have an attitude of what I call a "servant's heart."

The traditional management approach follows a top down style. Management gives directives for change. There is no serious attempt to get employee input. A more effective approach, figure one, is bottom up. Servant leaders understand that their employees have many good ideas as to how to be more effective. They work hard to determine what those ideas are and provide tools and training for best performance.

Servant Leadership

Management

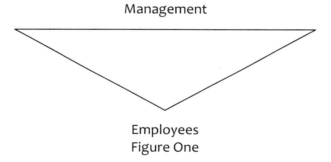

Employees
Figure One

Many leaders forget a basic adage of leadership, that is, their success depends on the success of others. Developer leaders understand that they contribute to the success of their employees by making it easier for them to do their jobs, by making them feel that their jobs have significant value and by treating them as individuals with valid opinions and suggestions.

A developer CEO understands that he needs to have significance in the lives of his employees. He understands the connection between performance and development and builds a culture that promotes and rewards personal growth.

Servant leadership at its most successful includes giving employees permission to take opportunities to create value for the organization as they work. Employees respond positively when you trust them and give them authority. They become the enthusiastic, motivated employees you want to develop.

Results of People Development

Research by Daniel Goleman, author of several books on Emotional Intelligence, finds that the organizational culture, the way people think about working for an organization, accounts for 20 to 30 percent of business performance.[2]

A specific validated example is customer service. Common wisdom is that employees who have a positive attitude will go the extra mile with customers.

There is a direct relationship to the bottom line. Goleman cites statistics that for every one percent in service improvement there is a two percent increase in revenue. [3]

Dramatic results can be achieved when we develop a performance culture focused on employee growth. When employees realize their personal goals as they help meet organizational goals great results are possible.

The impact on employees is impressive. As employees reach personal success they become positive and energized. Success breeds more success.

The effect of their success on the organization is infectious. Employee success leads to outstanding organizational success. The loftiest of company goals are reached more quickly with less effort.

Many organizations struggle with change as they try to adjust to the realities of their competitive environment. Successful people are impatient with the status quo. They understand how to effect change and proactively lead the organization to regular growth in revenue and profitability.

Developer CEOs understand that small improvements in personal effectiveness generate a much larger improvement in profitability. They know that personal involvement and leadership is required to get a positive return on their investment in people.

A Caveat

To build a development culture takes a leader with a positive belief in the basic nature of people. He believes people are motivated to achieve, desire self-fulfillment and seek responsibility.

---

[2] Daniel Goleman, *Primal Leadership*, Harvard Business School Press, 2002, page 107
[3] Ibid., page 15

He hires to these attributes. He sets a culture where these individuals can perform and expand their personal effectiveness.

A leader who doesn't have these attitudes may take personal control over tasks, be rules oriented and use punishment to control.

The developer leader understands the attitude that is required to build a performance culture. He becomes a leader with a "Servant's Heart," dedicating himself to the success of those who are helping him achieve his success.

An effective developer leader lives as a role model. "Do as I say not as I do" is not effective. Show the way by regularly increasing your effectiveness and celebrating your successes.

Summary

In today's pressure-packed business environment, management must quickly react to rapidly changing market conditions. A management team that works together to proactively effect change is a major organizational strength.

A key attitude of the CEO is to believe his people have a basic desire to improve themselves and to achieve at a high level. This "Developer" leader builds a performance culture.

The way people think about their company has a significant effect on their performance. There is a positive connection between the culture of the company and employee performance.

The developer CEO understands this. He encourages employees to create value for the company and customers as they do their jobs. He builds a culture where people can perform to their high standards and reach their personal goals. As they reach their goals, the company has equally outstanding success. Culture has a measurable impact on performance.

The culmination of a performance-based and employee-focused culture is competitive advantage in your marketplace.

All the ideas in this chapter relate to our personal leadership. If we are to build a results based culture we need to be effective leaders but if we can't lead ourselves how can we expect to lead our employees? We will explore this relationship in the next chapter.

Chapter 5 Best Ideas

Lead with a servant's heart.

Build a culture of enthusiastic, motivated, confident, grateful, committed people working together - with a high degree of cooperation and esprit de corps - on behalf of a future they have all committed themselves to.

My Best Ideas and Goals to Meet Them

_____

_____

_____

_____

_____

_____

6
Personal Leadership: A Key to Development

"Growth inside fuels growth outside."
John Maxwell

As we discussed in chapter five, personal development relates directly to profitability. Small improvements in personal effectiveness generate a much larger improvement in profitability.

Developer CEOs build a performance culture where people can perform to their high standards and reach their personal goals. As they reach their goals, the company has equally outstanding success.

The culmination of an employee-focused and performance-based culture is organizational excellence and competitive advantage in your marketplace.

Effective CEOs exhibit strong personal leadership. We need to lead others but if we can't lead ourselves how can we expect to lead our employees? In this chapter we will explore the relationship between performance and leadership.

51

What do Lee Iacocca and Bill Gates have in common? Certainly they were great leaders who knew what they wanted and how to get it.

However, they didn't succeed solely because they had great leadership qualities. They succeeded because they understood the importance of hiring managers who also possessed personal leadership skills. Hiring right is a crucial beginning.

These leaders continued building excellence by developing an environment in which leadership qualities flourished in all employees. As each employee reached new heights of achievement so did the organization, ensuring that the individuals and the organization outperformed the competition.

Leadership is an elusive trait. Large companies offer development to their managers through corporate universities. The typical CEO and senior management team of small to medium size companies don't have this advantage. They have little formal training in effective leadership and base their style on trial and error. This style is not effective. CEOs cannot lead others if they cannot effectively lead themselves. They must develop personal leadership in themselves and their management team.

Changing Attitudes toward Leadership

Whether a CEO, supervisor or employee, anyone can develop personal leadership and make it a dynamic force in his or her life.

Changing attitudes is difficult. Each of us has two things in common, the present and the future. During our present, we program our future. The program we set today determines the results we get tomorrow. If we desire to create a future that is different from our present, we must change our actions and the way we think today.

We exhibit personal leadership when we take responsibility for leading ourselves to reach our personal vision. We do this by changing our lives so that we reach new heights of achievement and lead a life that is positive and fulfilling.

Success Characteristics

The three characteristics of successful people are:
- **Goal direction**

They know where they stand, where they want to go and have a plan to get there.

- **Self motivation**
  As self starters, they wind their own clock.
- **Positive mental attitude**
  Successful people look for ways to complete tasks. They focus on strengths and break self-imposed limitations.

These traits are interrelated. Strengthen one and you strengthen them all. Success breeds success through increasing momentum.

Goal Direction

A much quoted study found that the three percent of the population who created a specific written plan became not only financially independent but out produced those with only general goals by 10 to 100 times.

Goal directed action leads to success, which arrives when you take that first step towards a goal, not when you reach your goal. Every action step you take towards your goal is a success that brings you closer to the end result you want.

You can learn the skill of goal direction. Effective CEOs provide goal training and instill goal direction in their organization. They ensure expected results when they hold themselves and their organization accountable.

When employees meet their personal goals while helping the company meet its goals, they make great achievements possible. Effective CEOs build an environment where personal and organizational goals complement each other.

Self-Motivation

Motivation, the sum of two words, motive and action, is the reason a person takes an action. Motivation, movement towards a goal, is a goal directed action.

In the business world, motivation often arises from fear or incentives, both of which are externally generated by another person and both of which are temporary in nature.

For instance, an employee might be scared by the threat of losing a bonus. Over time people build immunity to fear in that they work just hard enough to get the job done. They don't grow and develop to their full potential.

Incentives are often part of an employee's compensation plan. For example, a sales incentive plan can effectively increase sales in the short run. However, today's incentive plan often becomes tomorrow's expectation. As the reward becomes expected, the incentive must increase.

Self motivation, however, is internal, permanent and unique to each individual. We motivate ourselves. When we work and live through self-motivation, we take more control over our lives than we could ever imagine having, much like a thoroughbred horse that runs for the thrill of running. The joy and excitement of doing something we love brings great achievement and meaning to our lives. As we achieve and grow we build personal and organizational excellence.

Effective leaders understand that motivation is internal. They create a culture where people can achieve and grow.

Positive Mental Attitude

Which would you rather have as an employee or co-worker, a person with a positive attitude and average skills or a person with high skills and a negative attitude?

Effective leaders understand that attitude is everything. We heighten success when we look for ways to accomplish our goals rather than make excuses.

Winners and losers dress alike, eat in the same restaurants, shop in the same stores and work in the same offices. Attitude, behavior and the results they achieve make the difference.

Winners confidently expect that they can turn any situation to positive advantage. Using positive behaviors, they listen and learn. Their attitude and behavior lead to peak performance.

The difference between the average and very successful person is quite small. Successful people don't work three times as hard. Success is measured in inches. In baseball, the .300 hitter has only a small number of hits more than the .275 hitter but makes millions of dollars more.

Effective CEOs know how to develop the slight edge in people that creates a major increase in performance. They instill an attitude of abundance and positive expectance in their people.

The Most Important Leadership Attributes

The key to developing personal leadership is that you must believe in yourself first. Once you know you can accomplish anything you desire, you are ready to tackle the world and generate great personal success.

Even those not in management positions can begin to think like leaders. Position is unrelated to responsibility. Everyone who exhibits effective personal leadership and believes in themselves can become a leader and a positive role model.

The key leadership attributes are:

- Be a great role model. Forget the old adage, "Do as I say, not as I do." Your actions, not your words, are the most important messages that you send to others.
- Maintain a great attitude about people. Believe that your people are self directed and will work for personal growth and increased responsibility. Expect your staff to exhibit personal leadership and help them to continually grow to new levels.
- Be personally motivated. Be a thoroughbred that runs to win. You act to meet your personal needs and desires. Motivation is internal, not external.
- Inspire people to build their internal motivation by building motivation in yourself and by challenging everyone to be the best.
- Establish a regular personal improvement program. Improve even just 1% a month, a tiny amount. Through the miracle of compounding, you will double your effectiveness in about five years. This powerful motivator gives you control over your life and can double your effectiveness several times over during your career.
- Finally, work for yourself. Once you discover the great truth that your employer is paying you to work for yourself, you will realize that work is a blessing, not a burden. The better you hone your personal leadership skills, the more success you will bring to yourself.

Leaders achieve goals in cooperation with and through the actions of the people in their organization. Effective CEOs encourage their employees' personal success because they understand that personal success translates into organizational success. They know that successful people build successful organizations.

Summary

Personal leadership, whether at the CEO level or at the supervisory level, will bring you great personal rewards. You, as an effective personal leader, will develop a strong success attitude that gives you:

- The freedom to choose your own path to success.
- The confidence that you are following the life plan that is right for you.
- The elimination of confusion and frustration that comes from trying to please others.
- The challenge and excitement of developing all of your own potential.

Strong personal leadership also gives the organization a competitive advantage in today's compressed, highly competitive business cycle.

Growth is a great separator for success. As we grow inside, the reward is what we become. Growth is not automatic. Have a personal growth plan that you regularly work on in your personal HPA.

The difference between being average and successful is small. A successful person doesn't work harder, he or she works with a distinct goal in mind. For this reason effective CEOs strive to strengthen success traits in themselves and their employees.

Personal and organizational successes go together. When employees meet their personal goals as they help the organization meet its goals, they make great achievements possible. Effective CEOs build an environment where personal and organizational goals complement each other.

Effective CEOs take the attitude for themselves and their management team that "If you don't grow, you go." They understand that when they exhibit personal leadership as they strive to evolve the organization to the next level, they also provide a role model for their employees, who must accept and lead change.

In the resulting culture, employees meet their personal goals by helping the organization meet its goals. Personal growth translates into organizational success.

Chapter 6 Best Ideas

Personal leadership is a prerequisite for effective organizational leadership.

Leadership attitudes drive personal success.

Build success traits in employees for competitive advantage.

My Best Ideas and Goals to Meet Them

_____

_____

_____

_____

_____

_____

7
Organizational Leadership for Effective Development

"The price of greatness is responsibility."
Winston Churchill

In Chapter 6 we explored the importance of personal leadership as a prerequisite for organizational excellence. With this foundation we are ready to provide effective leadership to our organization.

You don't compound success by doing what you personally can do. You compound success by bringing others to your vision and accomplishing that vision through them.

Myth of Individualism

Many leaders think they can do it all. They built their organization to current levels by trusting their abilities and instincts and see no reason to change what worked for them. They lead others by controlling work output.

Then they reach a plateau. No matter how hard they try, they fail to rise to the next level. They have forgotten the definition of insanity: they repeat the same processes and expect different results.

The most effective leaders understand that they are expert in some areas critical to their business. They also understand that they do not need to be expert in all areas and that doing everything themselves limits their potential for success. They lead by letting go of control.

Why do we have such a hard time accepting the fact that our success depends on relationships and alliances with others as much as it does on ourselves?

We let the "Myth of Individualism," the idea that everyone succeeds or fails based on individual effort and ability, lead us astray.

From the earliest days of colonial exploration to the settling of the Wild West, to the present day, we have made individualism a strong part of our culture.

We glorify the myth in our literature, television and movies. Our earliest authors wrote about the successes of the pioneers. Zane Grey's protagonists succeeded against overwhelming odds. One hero, The Lone Ranger, is even appropriately named. To this day action heroes on television and in movies perpetuate the myth of individualism.

This myth is so powerful that when experts suggest the alternative idea that success depends on relationships with others as much as it does on us, we resist accepting it.

Emotional Intelligence as a Leadership Style

The developer CEO leads with a servant's heart and shares power with his management team. He uses emotional intelligence effectively to create an organization where people want to be and want to do their best; an organization in resonance. He is intelligent about emotions both within himself and his employees.

Daniel Goleman, PhD, gave Emotional Intelligence its name and organized it into a coherent subject. EI, being intelligent about emotions, is a different way of being smart than IQ or book smarts.

Emotional intelligence is a key factor in leadership success. Leaders need to create resonance – as opposed to dissonance – to create a positive environment that frees people to do their best.

Most of us have an intuitive feel that IQ and success do not have a high correlation. We can all cite examples of people who were very IQ intelligent but not very successful in business. Others with average intelligence outperformed them. What was the difference? The high performers created an organization that was in resonance.

Goleman breaks EI competencies into two areas. The first is intra personal - personal competence. The second is inter-personal - social competence. See Appendix Three for the complete list.

It is not necessary to have strengths in all competencies. Highly effective leaders exhibit a critical mass of strengths in about six competencies that are important to their profession and to them personally. Since there are many paths to excellence in every profession, these are not always the same for everyone.

Personal competencies provide the basic groundwork but social competencies set the effective leader apart.

In Chapter 6 we discussed traits of successful people: positive mental attitude, self motivation and goal direction. These are key to personal competence in EI. Positive mental attitude is the self-confidence competency in self awareness. Self motivation and goal direction are the self-management competencies of achievement and initiative.

All leaders compound success by developing people focus. Inter-personal social competencies are fundamental for this success. Empathy, the understanding of others, is the fundamental social competency and is the foundation skill for all other social competencies.

People with this competency:
- Are attentive to emotional cues and listen well
- Show sensitivity and understand others' perspectives
- Help based on understanding of other people's needs and feelings
- Are great communicators with employees, suppliers and customers

Empathy ties in with the other social competencies and encompasses:

Understanding others: Sensing others' perspectives and feelings and taking an active interest in their concerns.

Service orientation: Anticipating, recognizing and meeting customers' needs.

Political awareness: Reading the political and social currents in an organization. This involves being able to read the tea leaves and understand how the political climate affects people's ability to perform.

Developing others: Empathy is sensing others' development needs and bolstering their abilities.

There are three levels of empathy:

- Being able to read another's emotions
- Sensing and responding to a person's unspoken concerns or feelings.
- Understanding the issues or concerns that lie behind another's feelings.

We develop empathy through:

- Listening
- Questioning
- Communicating

A finely tuned ear is at the heart of empathy. The key to developing empathy is listening for what's important to others and their success. Listening well is essential. Techniques to use for effective listening include:

- Look people in the eye - focus on them.
- Smile – a smile is the shortest distance between two people.
- Think about what they are saying not what you are going to say next.

Listening well goes beyond hearing what is said. Active listening is about asking questions to probe and clarify the information you have heard and to go into unspoken areas.

Listening is about communicating your thoughts effectively. It's effective give and take. It's about registering the emotional clues you see and hear and tuning your message to seek mutual understanding. If you understand where the other person is coming from, you can match your message to them.

How to Build Success Traits

Effective CEOs use these four action steps to build success traits in their management team:

- **Create a positive work environment.**
    People respond to their environment. Build an environment where people want to be and want to do their best.
- **Encourage stretching for professional development.**
    Most people want to progress and grow. Effective leaders make a point of learning what motivates their employees and then give personal and organizational encouragement.
- **Strive for excellence.**
    Help people hold themselves accountable for their personal goals. Hold them accountable for organizational goals.
- **Share power with your management team.**
    Understand that sharing power is the most effective way to build personal motivation. When participants take intellectual and emotional ownership of the initiative, they become part of the solution and develop personal commitment to the outcome.

How to Build Self Esteem

Effective leaders understand that attitude is crucial and that self esteem, the sum of our conditioning from an early age, affects it in many ways. Leaders raise the self esteem of their employees by helping them:

- **Avoid comparison to others.**
    When we compare ourselves to others we set ourselves up for disappointment. Someone always has stronger experience. The only relevant measure of personal improvement is to compare our capabilities from yesterday to our capabilities today.
- **Resist putting yourself down.**
    Don't let the person in the mirror become a block. Understand your starting point and set a goal to change.

Once you start to actively work towards a goal, you create success not at the end point but during the game. Every day you work towards the culmination of your long range goals.

- **Improve a discipline in some part of your life.**
  Working to fulfill your goals gives you an incentive to do more and do it better each day. When you consistently take the right actions, you feel better about yourself and regularly reach a higher plateau.

- **Celebrate small victories.**
  Recognize that each step you complete towards your goals is a positive accomplishment that takes you closer to your final objective. You raise your effectiveness every day.

Summary

The successful leader with his management team has developed a vision for the organization. His HPA is to help all employees understand how their job relates to the company vision and help them reach their goals as the company reaches its goals. In this environment great success is possible. Visionary and effective leadership brings competitive advantage.

Developer leaders don't go it alone. They compound success by sharing power and working effectively through their employees. They understand that success depends on their relationships with others as much as it does on them.

Developer leaders continually build their and their management team's leadership effectiveness.

In the next chapter we discuss how to build the traits we need to succeed.

Chapter 7 Best Ideas

Build organizational resonance and a positive environment.

Develop Emotional Intelligence competencies to enhance your effectiveness.

Build success traits and self esteem for organizational success.

My Best Ideas and Goals to Meet Them

_____

_____

_____

_____

_____

_____

_____

8
Third Mistake: Lack of Practice

**"We are what we repeatedly do;
excellence, then, is not an act, but a habit."
Aristotle**

We all know we want personal successes from our jobs, such as reaching a certain sales level or getting that major promotion. We work toward these successes by regularly practicing skills, behaviors and traits that lead to higher effectiveness.

When we concentrate on fulfillment of our goals, we give ourselves a reason to do more and do it better every day. We regularly reach higher plateaus and develop a can do attitude. Success breeds more success, leading to our becoming the successful person we envision.

Effective CEOs build a culture where employees can become personal successes because they understand that successful people build successful organizations.

Practice

Successful people always search for and acquire knowledge that will make them more effective. Knowledge is the key. Without it nobody can go to the next level.

However, we must use the knowledge we gain for it to become valuable. A favorite saying of mine is, "No great manager or leader ever fell from heaven. It is a learned skill, not inherited." To enhance our success we must practice regularly to internalize the knowledge we've gained.

Personal development doesn't come without sustained effort and commitment. It takes about six weeks of regular practice to master even simple new skills.

Tiger Woods is the top professional in his field. He may hit a thousand practice shots for every tournament shot. He practices regularly and performs periodically. We in the business world are just the opposite. We perform every day but rarely practice.

We hear about a new technique and try to use it immediately, failing to realize that it may take thousands of hours of practice, practice, practice and substantial effort to become comfortable with it. Before we implement a new technique, we must devote time to becoming experts in its use. The key to developing new habits lies in practice to the point of mastery.

When we don't practice we get in a rut, defined as, "A coffin with the ends knocked out," and never develop our potential or the potential of our organization. We fall into the insanity trap when we do the same things over and over and expect different results. We recycle our problems!

Identify Your Areas for Improvement

Let's personalize this discussion. In Chapter 6 we talked about personal leadership. Effective leadership traits are behavioral in nature. We must change the way we interact with others if we are to be successful. To be successful we need to become proficient in those behaviors that will further our success. We h ave to DO. Understanding is not enough.

Marshall Goldsmith in his book *What Got You Here Won't Get You There* identifies twenty common interpersonal behavior and leadership flaws performed by one person against another. See Appendix Four for the complete list.

Two examples are:

- Many of us could become more effective communicators. Effective communication is a competitive advantage in most areas of our lives.
- Feeling appreciated is a basic human need. How many of us regularly compliment our co-workers or employees? Are we so focused on our problems and initiatives that we fail to notice the efforts of others?

We also have personal behaviors that inhibit our leadership capabilities. These are behaviors that have a direct relationship to professional success. They are the way we respond every day to our workplace.

Three examples are:

- Naturally reserved people could become more effective if they could develop the capability to be more at ease when the situation warranted.
- Many managers lack the ability to effectively delegate routine tasks. They end up doing such tasks instead of more important work that would generate higher success.
- Work with people to get their personal commitment rather than dictate what we want and how we will get there.

With these suggestions and your thoughts from previous chapters as a basis, take a few moments to write the behaviors you would like to strengthen and identify an action plan to develop them.

_____

_____

_____

_____

_____

_____

Your Personal Plan

The good news is we can improve our behavior traits. The bad news is it takes time and effort. Tiger Woods became who he is only through many years of focused practice.

Research tells us it can take up to 5,000 hours of practice to become expert. If it takes this long, why do we ever start?

The answer is twofold. The rewards of achieving competitive advantage and sustainable results are too important for us to not improve our personal effectiveness.

Second, research by Goleman and others finds that the journey we take to make improvements is incremental. We don't have to wait for 5,000 hours to become more effective. We improve our capabilities continually. Most important, we retain our changes. The 1% attitude is continuous and life changing.

The following seven steps have proven effective in making behavioral changes become permanent. They reflect common sense and are easy to understand. They are also hard to put into effect because they require discipline and persistence.

#1 Think transformation, not training. Our present is the sum total of our actions and the way we think. If we want to reach a different future we need to change our behaviors and thoughts. Think about improving effectiveness, not just skills. Yes, skills are important but as we progress in management we become more effective by working through people.

#2 Determine where you are now. The most successful leaders have strong self-awareness and self-confidence along with a deep understanding of their emotions, strengths, limitations, values and motives. They are realistic and honest with themselves and about themselves. They know where they are headed and why. This applies equally to your key employees.

One technique is to use assessments to give good in depth non-judgmental evaluation. All assessments describe. Some diagnose and the best can be used for people development.

It is important to assess your organization as well. The key in both areas is to be realistic. Now is not the time to rationalize or convince yourself that the situation is different from what it truly is.

This is a good area to build alliances. Most managers do not have experience using assessments. They are too close to the issue and may not be objective. Build an alliance with an experienced professional who understands high level assessments. He will give you an unbiased opinion.

#3 Determine where you want to go. Your vision – your burning desire – has to be well-conceived. Develop a personal vision and review it periodically. Your vision will change as you mature and achieve success.

#4 Define the gap. This is the difference between where you are now and where you want to be. Determine how you will measure what you want to accomplish so you can determine how you are progressing.

#5 Have a written plan. It is important to put your plan in writing. Writing crystallizes your thoughts. The discipline of writing it down will help focus you. Write down your vision, where you are now, where you want to be and the gap.

#6 Start taking action. It's not necessary to know all the details in advance. Decisive people think this way: I'm going to start pending working out all the details. Contrast this to less successful people who think that once they've worked out all the details they will start.

#7 Hold yourself accountable. "Inspect what you expect." Write your plan's action steps into your schedule. If you don't schedule your activities, daily "urgent" matters will take precedence and you will slip.

Summary

Global competition and rapidly changing technology are constant challenges. If we want to develop competitive advantage, we must continually improve our effectiveness.

Practice is important to our success, otherwise we fall into the insanity trap and end up in a rut; "a coffin with the ends knocked out."

Build a culture where employees reach their goals as they help the company reach its goals. Build accountability for improvements into the culture of the organization. For best results become a role model for others.

You must take action. Take time each day to plan, implement your plan, and review your progress. Make adjustments as needed. When you do this frequently you will maintain the pace you have set and see continuous personal improvement.

Success breeds more success. As you see improvement, you become energized, self-motivated and build your positive mental attitude.

Chapter 8 Best Ideas

Build a plan to make behavioral change.

Practice, practice, practice.

Schedule time to practice.

My Best Ideas and Goals to Meet Them

_____

_____

_____

_____

_____

_____

9
Fourth Mistake: Lack of Planning

"Failing to plan is planning to fail."
John Wooden

CEOs of small to medium sized companies often do not plan effectively. If they have a vision for the future, it is poorly defined and is not the product of the best thinking of the management team. Their plans all too often change on whims.

Successful CEOs understand that strategic planning using the combined experience, education and perspectives of the management team is a highly effective means of developing focus in management and competitive advantage in the marketplace. In this chapter we will discuss strategic planning. In the next chapter we will discuss utilizing best thinking as an effective tool to develop the most complete strategic plan.

Patrick Below states, "Strategic planning is the most important activity a CEO and his management team can undertake." Effective planning focuses the team. Focus drives performance and performance drives results. Effective planning will produce consistent results. Profitability and revenue will increase year after year.

One study of small to medium sized companies with equal capabilities, Figure One, demonstrates the importance of planning. Companies with equal capabilities in the same industry with and without planning had vastly different results. Those with plans significantly out-performed less well managed organizations. Companies with strategic plans were 40% larger than those without such plans, had slightly fewer workers and thus, 45% higher revenues per employee.

Figure One

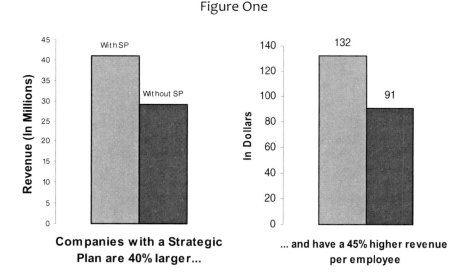

Companies with a Strategic Plan are 40% larger...

... and have a 45% higher revenue per employee

The clear message is that strategic planning produces competitive advantage in your marketplace.

Large companies have departments devoted to strategic analysis and planning. Small to medium sized companies don't understand the value of planning and don't plan. Typically the CEO of a smaller company admits, "We are too busy generating revenue day-to-day and don't have the time for planning."

The business environment has changed significantly. Faced with continual change, CEOs find it difficult to drive their companies to deliver sustainable results. As a result, companies have far less time to react and place themselves at a tremendous disadvantage when they focus only on the short term.

Strategic Plan

A simple, clear definition of a strategic plan is: a thorough, concise, roadmap of a desired vision for the organization at a specific time in the future. Effective strategic planning focuses the management team. The purpose of a good plan is to produce sustainable results on a continuous basis.

A strategic plan is the basic foundation of the company, providing a concrete frame of reference for making decisions about how to compete in the marketplace. It includes a clear outline of the functional assets, financial assets and system requirements needed to achieve the plan.

Example: Strategic Plan

In 2002 a residential construction framing business had about 50 employees and revenues of $2.0 million per year. Management identified three key areas as industry success factors: pre-planning projects, enhanced customer service and high quality training of framers. The company developed a strategic plan to develop these into core competencies.

Through executing their plan the company developed strong core competencies in comprehensive project planning, exceptional service to the prime contractor and subs and effective employee training. These contributed to outstanding efficiency and quality.

Four years later the company generated revenues of $34 million with over 250 employees. The company's industry reputation now precedes them with primes seeking them to work on their jobs.

Strategic thinking leads the company to consider the business from the point of view of the customer's reasons for buying products or services. A strategic plan identifies the key success factors the company needs to implement to achieve plan goals and identifies how to develop these into core competencies.

Strategic planning isn't about tactics. It is the fundamental thinking behind other plans and must not be confused with an operational plan, which states where the company is now and where it is going.

Vision

A corporate vision is a necessary first step in a strategic plan. Effective CEOs recognize that their organization's vision provides a basic foundation. A vision is a clear inspirational statement of where the company will be in the future.

When employees understand and internalize the vision, they become emotionally involved in the company's direction. Employees that are committed to the company vision are more effective in their jobs. A well crafted vision is a foundation for organizational values and a performance based culture.

A concise vision is effective with customers and suppliers. It sets their expectations of your organization, communicates your values and helps establish the basis of your relationship with them.

Effective Planning Model

The CEO must balance day-to-day issues and long term vision, which are not mutually exclusive. While daily productivity, short term results and generating revenue are important, effective planning allows the organization to proactively respond to longer term market changes. The CEO must give both short and long term issues the proper emphasis for the organization to truly prosper.

The most successful organizations use a planning model that integrates short and long term needs, creating an effective planning process that produces consistent sustainable results over time.

The model in Figure 2 shows all three areas: the strategic plan, the operational plan and results management, integrated into a framework that drives results towards the long term vision of the organization. This model integrates both processes of finding where the company wants to go and how it will get there.

Integrated Planning Process		
STRATEGIC PLANNING	OPERATIONAL PLANNING	RESULTS MANAGEMENT
Vision, Mission & Values	Operational Analysis	Control Systems
Strategic Analysis	Key Results Areas	Management Reports
Strategy Statement	Performance Indicators	Organizational Results
Strategic Objectives	Operational Objective	Individual Results
Financial Projections	Action Plans	Corrective Action
People Development	Budgets	Reward Systems

Integrated Planning Process © 2003 The Executive Guide to Strategic Planning, by Patrick J. Below, George L. Morrisey, Betty L. Acomb (Jossey Bass), 1987

Figure Two

The integrated process starts with strategic analysis and usually focuses three to five years into the future. We evaluate what business our organization is in and how to position it to get where we want to be. A detailed analysis of the past provides a starting point for decisions about the future. The plan covers both external and internal aspects, determining the key success factors in each market segment and within the organization. Management evaluates performance against these benchmarks and determines the gap between where the company is now and where it wants to be. The key is to identify how to turn these success factors into core competencies.

Operational planning identifies the results that implementation of the strategic plan will produce during that year. An operational plan works best when it crosses functional areas, requiring the input and coordination of several departments. This breaks down departmental silos and develops stronger organizational teamwork.

While senior management usually does strategic planning, operational planning should include lower levels of the organization.

Focusing on the issues throughout the organization ensures wide commitment from key people.

Plans often fall behind in execution. Continuous effort is crucial to results management. Every day short term priorities take management time and delay results. Management must use focused discipline to regularly monitor and control progress.

The effective CEO understands the importance of active involvement by everyone in the planning process. His personal high payoff activity is to challenge his team to think more strategically every day.

In this model, the management team develops the plan. When the team takes responsibility for thinking through and completing the analysis, it owns the plan. Successful CEOs understand that they must personally commit to this success and drive the process.

Assess Your Planning Process

We all plan to some degree already. Assess your current planning process and compare it to the integrated planning model. Use these questions as thought starters and idea generators.

- In past planning processes, what worked well? What should you have built upon and continued? What didn't work well and should be improved?
- In terms of your organization's performance in the past fiscal year, what are the biggest lessons you learned that can improve performance during the next fiscal year?
- What do you consider to be the two or three most important organizational priorities for the next fiscal year?
- In your view, how can the organization do a better job of understanding and meeting the needs of your various markets?
- How can you improve growth during the next one to three years using a more robust planning process?

To determine your planning gap, evaluate the effectiveness of your current practice compared to the best practice as defined in the integrated planning model. If your gap is large, you should explore how to better utilize planning to focus you and your team.

Focus On the Big Picture

Small to medium sized companies face pervasive competition. Due to their size there is little they can do to affect their market. Competition can get bloody, particularly when the competitor has a production cost advantage. Whether you have a proprietary product or are a subcontractor, there often is not much differentiation between companies in a competitive environment.

In this situation develop value innovation as a differentiator.

Example: Objectives

Flower pots provide an example. Home Depot and other big box retailers sell pots in their lawn and garden departments.

In the last ten years pot production has moved from the US to Asia due to lower production cost. The purchasing department buys pots primarily on price.

Store management has different objectives. They focus on inventory, sales turns and shrinkage. They want product that sells at regular price, not product that requires massive write downs at the end of the season.

Product from Asia does not match US product in design, uniform quality or weight. Weight is particularly important. Women are the primary purchasers of pots. In the larger sizes, pots from Asia can weigh up to 70 pounds. US pots of similar size weigh 35 pounds. When weight is combined with design and quality, women greatly prefer US pots. Weight is an effective value proposition.

Unfortunately, the small US companies in this industry have all succumbed to foreign competition and 99% of the pots sold in the domestic market are foreign made.

Often we focus on the same buyer group as our competitors and define products and services similarly. When a clear differentiation between us and our competitors does not exist, we need look past traditional market boundaries, even with current customers. When we understand our customers' key success factors, we can better determine which factors lead to customers' decisions to buy. We make their key success factors our core competencies.

How many of you know your customer's needs and perceptions? How many of you visit customers to find out first hand what is important to them?

Most companies usually communicate with the purchasing department, which mostly focuses on price and delivery. These purchasing department objectives are often different from those of the end user, whose relevant needs include inventory, quality, engineering, and design changes.

Executing Strategy

Executing strategy in a small to medium sized company can be difficult. All of us are comfortable with the status quo. However, we must get people to realize that change is necessary. When we determine that our company performance is weak, a shocking but actionable problem, we must convince our employees to quickly remedy the situation. By the time we have gone from 200 employees to 100, it is too late.

Financial resources are often a problem. Small companies don't have the capital reserves of larger organizations. As revenue goes down this gap becomes even larger. In addition, capital often comes from the personal reserves of the company leaders.

The obvious solution is to generate more dollars. Equally obvious is that this isn't easy and most options are undesirable. One effective solution is to multiply the resources you already control. Evaluate your operations for spending that has little impact on performance and for those activities that have the greatest impact on performance but are financially starved. Thinking this way gives you insight into how to free up money spent on low-return resources and redirect those funds to higher impact uses.

In Chapter 3 we discussed change. Change doesn't come easily. In accomplishing change, small and medium sized companies have an advantage over larger organizations. Both have similar issues when bringing about change. However, CEOs of large companies have tens of thousands of employees spread over many locations. Smaller companies have only hundreds of employees at one or two locations.

Concentrate your change efforts on the key people in your company. First get them committed to the change initiative and build their self motivation. Now you and your key people can use that combined strength to build trust and commitment in all employees and overcome resisters. This method is easier when used to implement change in a smaller organization.

Finally, have a distinct results management process. If you don't, your plan will slip since generating revenue on a daily basis will dominate your time.

Summary

Strategic planning is fundamental to developing competitive advantage.

In today's challenging business environment companies must proactively react to change or be left behind. As the example of international price competition demonstrates, these changes are often not just directional but transformational.

The effective CEO doesn't look at strategic planning as a discrete event to be accomplished periodically. The CEO's highest payoff activity is to embed strategic thinking into everyday management thinking. He asks, "What can my team and I do to think more strategically every day?"

The integrated planning process defines best practice in strategic planning. Many plans fail to some degree because the three key areas outlined in Figure 2 are not integrated into a coordinated process. Plans often fail to fulfill their potential in each of the three categories because:

- No true strategic analysis and thinking is conducted.
- Annual budgeting is considered planning. Budgeting is not even a comprehensive operational plan.
- There is no regular effective results management process.

Planning that has active management participation in all its phases is the most important activity a CEO and his team can undertake. Organizations that follow the integrated planning process raise their effectiveness to a level that can't be reached by any other means. The focus they develop generates competitive advantage in their marketplace.

Since successful CEOs want to generate sustainable results over time, they use effective planning to focus their efforts on the right activities, which greatly improves the opportunity for success.

Chapter 9 Best Ideas

Planning provides competitive advantage.

Results management is imperative for sustainable results.

Building strategic thinking in the management team is a HPA.

My Best Ideas and Goals to Meet Them

_____

_____

_____

_____

_____

_____

10
Best Thinking: A Key To Effective Planning

"None of us is as smart as all of us."
Ken Blanchard

Companies that plan may have up to 45% higher revenue than competitors of equal size and capability. If planning is this important to our competitive position, it is to our advantage to use all the capability available to us. Best thinking is an effective tool to develop the most complete strategic plan.

Best thinking is personal and organizational. Personal best thinking is the basis for great organizational best thinking.

Personal Best Thinking

We have all experienced that "AHA" moment when we connected an idea we had struggled to understand with an experience that made the idea perfectly clear. This experiential learning process is fundamental to best thinking.

Those who develop best thinking become experts in their fields. They gain increasing esteem from their peers and a confidence level that places them at the top of their profession. Best thinking becomes an attitude of continuous discovery. Best thinkers don't segment their thinking into periodic events. They make strategic thinking a regular process.

People who take best thinking to its highest level interact with others who have a mutual desire to share knowledge, education, experience and wisdom with one another. A burst of creativity flows from the combined energies and intellects of those who share experiences and build from a combined base.

When this happens, the participants create knowledge greater than the sum of the parts, a case where two plus two can truly become five. Everyone involved raises their personal effectiveness to a higher level than they could achieve by themselves.

When we strive to become experts in our field, we build expertise through formal education and practical experience. Over time, experiential learning allows us to effectively apply our knowledge to a wide variety of situations. At this level of best thinking, our educational gaps, innate ability, and personal biases constrict our expertise, keeping our learning one dimensional. We need more knowledge and experience than we possess but often fail to recognize that need.

It comes as a surprise to many people that when they build increased experience and knowledge through interaction with other professionals, they raise their best thinking to a level they never expected to achieve.

This highest level of best thinking happens because group interaction supports expanded creative thinking. We build our expertise on a far wider base of education and experience than we could have attained by ourselves. We rise above our personal limitations and biases. Individual gems of wisdom and experience combine to form a creative base of practical knowledge.

Effective Attitudes for Personal Best Thinking

To embrace best thinking, professionals need to adjust their attitudes and behaviors.

Best thinking is a continual process, not an event. We must develop an "I'm always learning" mentality. John Wooden said it very concisely, "It's what we learn after we know it all that counts."

We cannot wait for the annual convention. We must make regular dialogue with others a way of life. When we notice and remember the little gems of wisdom we get from others, experiential learning happens, giving us "AHA" moments and great leaps ahead in our thinking.

When we share with others, we need a strong sense of self and a positive mental attitude, which allows us to interact comfortably with others and to accept them even when they have very different ideas. People with strong self-awareness understand their emotions, strengths, limitations, values and motives at a deep level. They are honest with themselves about themselves. They know the direction they want their life to take and why.

When we ask others to participate with us in a dialog about our projects and concerns, we must share with them. These wide-ranging, in-depth creative discussions must involve give and take between the two parties for the absolute best thinking to take place.

To develop a strong give and take relationship, become significant in the lives of others. People with significance understand that they contribute to the success of others. They ask, "How can I help you?" They dedicate their time and energy to the success of those who help them achieve their success. When you get others to realize that you truly care about them and have their best interests at heart, you will have created a relationship that fosters best thinking.

In contrast, the self-centered person loses the opportunity to develop the highest level of best thinking because he focuses too much on himself, making it difficult for others to interact with him. He does not have the give and take attitude necessary for interpersonal dialog.

You must be non-judgmental when you interact with others. Accept others for what they can contribute. Don't force your values and expectations on them. Don't expect more than they can give. Be open to all contributions.

When you engage in open-ended discussions, use the creative right side of your brain. You will discover that no wrong answers exist and that everything is possible. The more ideas you develop the better. You can later use the left side of your brain to analyze the ideas you have created.

Organizational Best Thinking

Wise leaders know that they will generate organizational best thinking that is far above what one person can accomplish alone when they draw on the wealth of knowledge that employees, with their differing professional interests, experiences and perspectives, bring to their jobs.

Best thinking is a catalyst that:

- Raises the effectiveness of an organization to a level that cannot be reached by any other means.
- Builds personal motivation among team members by allowing them to personally contribute both emotionally and intellectually.
- Develops focus in organizational direction and initiatives.
- Brings members of management teams together so that they become change agents, not change critics, working together for the good of the company.

Companies and executives that use best thinking understand that it is a level above consensus. The collective experience is tapped for maximum creativity. Best thinking brings competitive advantage and this advantage flows directly to the bottom line.

Best thinking is not a natural function in most organizations. The most common organizational structure has functional areas that operate as vertical silos. Managers are responsible for their silo and management is hierarchical. It is natural for employees in each silo to think their work is the most important.

How can effective leaders develop best thinking?

Change starts with the CEO, and the leadership of the organization. Effective leaders are personally aware. They also have a strong awareness of the organization. They know how employees view the organizational structure, leadership style and culture. They make a conscious effort to resolve differences between the ideal and employee perceptions.

Their personal attitude and organizational knowledge allow CEOs to share power with employees as they guide and inspire them with a compelling vision. Effective leaders develop high-level, cross-functional best thinking that crosses boundaries and helps expand employee attitudes.

CEOs must trust their management team to carry out their vision. Great leaders learn how to inspire people. When they spend the time to fully develop a team they gain confidence in the team's ability to work together and achieve results.

Where is best thinking most effective in an organization?

Historically companies have used planning and best thinking on a sporadic basis, sending team members back to their silos and their compartmentalized jobs after short brainstorming sessions. These irregular events fail to build best thinking into the everyday consciousness of employees.

For instance, the management team may apply best thinking only at infrequent strategic planning sessions where the management team together plans the direction of the company.

CEOs who wish to develop an environment where shared knowledge becomes part of the culture of the company must build best thinking into the organization on an everyday basis.

Best thinking is appropriate in all planning activities and in every functional area. For instance, in new product development a team encompassing best thinking would receive input from engineering, marketing, sales and production. In manufacturing, inventory planning would receive input from finance, marketing, sales and production.

What are the barriers to best thinking?

The most common barriers to best thinking are:

- Lack of commitment and focus from the CEO.
- Organizational political realities wherein people develop judgments and patterns of working that block open communication.
- A perception among employees that their work ranks first among all tasks.

- Lack of expertise among leaders at achieving open, out of the box dialog from a diverse group.

How can companies build best thinking practices?

Building organizational best thinking practices takes commitment and focus from the CEO, who must encourage employees to work and interact together.

Best thinking takes time to develop. Initial thoughts are always fragile and not fully formed. In planning sessions CEOs must allow the time and open dialog necessary for these initial thoughts to fully develop into best thinking. If the company environment is not conducive to open, honest dialog without fear, best thinking will not happen.

Organizational best thinking is most effective when it becomes part of the culture and is ingrained in employees' attitudes. Many CEOs start this process by building cross-functional teams that they charge with specific initiatives. These teams can operate at different levels in the organization and work on issues that are appropriate to their level of responsibility. CEOs hold these teams accountable for developing functionally integrated responses to everyday business issues.

Summary

Since successful CEOs want to generate sustainable results over time, they use effective planning to focus their efforts on the right activities, which greatly improves the opportunity for success.

Building personal best thinking is a positive leadership trait of the effective leader. When you communicate with others on a continuous basis, you develop and maintain your status as an expert in your field. You will achieve "AHA" moments by being non-judgmental and remembering that everything is possible. Nurture a mind open to all ideas.

Develop a strong sense of self-awareness and confidence. You will be more genuine and open with others when you have confidence in your own abilities and ideas.

Develop significance in the lives of others. You will foster the highest level of best thinking when others realize that you are giving your time and energy to their success and they can contribute to yours.

The combined organizational best thinking of the team rises to a very high level as the planning process draws on the wealth of knowledge that employees, with differing professional interests, experiences and perspectives, bring to their jobs.

Best thinking must drive all planning events, which are too important for anything but the best efforts of all members of the management team. CEOs must incorporate best thinking into the culture of the business so employees regularly share knowledge across functional boundaries.

Properly implemented best thinking is the catalyst that generates high level focus. Focus drives performance and performance drives results.

Companies with high level best thinking are larger, leaner and more profitable. Best thinking becomes the catalyst for competitive advantage.

Best thinking is genius work – one of the highest and best uses of the CEO's time.

Chapter 10 Best Ideas

Organizational best thinking brings the highest level of success.

Best thinking is a positive leadership trait.

Open dialog brings AHA experiences.

My Best Ideas and Goals to Meet Them

_____

_____

_____

_____

_____

_____

11
Fifth Mistake: Lack of Accountability

"Inspect what you expect."
Anon

Have you participated in a business initiative that your company never completed? Have you watched key business goals suffer as teams missed deadline after deadline?

Often such problems arise because neither the employees nor the management team hold themselves truly accountable. When teams don't execute effectively because of a lack of accountability, the company fails to generate results.

Accountability for results is the crucial step in producing outstanding performance. The CEO is responsible for creating accountability in his organization. Many CEOs have trouble eliciting this accountability.

CEOs and executives often don't hold themselves and their organizations accountable. They don't execute well in two distinct areas: regular daily activities and strategic planning initiatives.

To a great extent accountability in these two areas can be mutually exclusive.

Accountability for Generating Revenue

Accountability often is not built into our regular daily management functions. We try to focus on generating revenue but have a hard time effectively accomplishing this. How many of us have a see-saw production schedule where much of our revenue is generated in the last days of the accounting period? This revenue is only generated with higher overtime and other costs.

Daily accountability has to do with people productivity. In Chapter 2 we discussed efficiency and effectiveness. Many people focus on efficiency. It is more important that we focus on effectiveness. The HPA of management is to drive effectiveness and people productivity.

HPA provide the framework to accountability. We establish a SMART goal, define action steps with clear responsibilities and get them on our schedule and the schedules of our team. Accountability comes when we "inspect what we expect." Because we are regularly monitoring progress, if we slip an action step, we have just a small correction to make to return to our original timetable.

This process doesn't have to take substantial time. People become used to reporting progress. They dislike standing in front of peers and giving excuses for lack of performance. The culture of accountability and performance becomes routine.

Accountability for regular performance is basic to success and important to the performance of the management team.

Accountability in Strategic Planning

As we explored in Chapter 9, planning generates competitive advantage. However, planning in a vacuum is ineffective. The purpose of planning is to develop consistent results. To be effective the planning process needs to have a results management phase. There needs to be accountability.

First, the CEO and his management team must develop and commit to a clear vision and translate that vision into a coordinated strategic plan. Without this foundation, everyday pressures will overwhelm the process, producing an ever-changing environment that causes indecision and delays.

Second, the management team must make certain that everyone within the company knows that it is committed to the initiative. When teams work under public scrutiny, they develop a strong desire to succeed and to share the achievement. Teams that only commit to doing well are subtly preparing for eventual failure.

Third, the team must place the organization above individual interests. When individuals channel their efforts into making the team work better, positive results occur. Conversely, when individuals protect their turf and work at cross purposes, they doom the initiative.

Fourth, team members must coordinate their high payoff activities so they work with the same result in mind. The team must focus both individually and collectively on objectives and outcomes to generate positive performance.

Using Accountability to Generate Results

It is not enough to establish accountability in a company. To create results, management must decide how to measure performance. Revenue and profit goals are important but beyond that management must clearly identify relevant metrics, ensure that those metrics are realistic, and specify expected completion dates.

Any objective can be measured. Some may take more effort to determine effective measurements than others. Revenue and other quantitative measurements that automatically come from accounting information are easy. Other measurements such as job cost, shrinkage and inventory variances can come from the accounting system with only a little additional effort.

Qualitative measurements are more difficult. First we must determine what metrics are really representative of the objective we are looking to measure. Then we must figure out how to generate the information from our management systems.

Effective CEOs understand that projects never go as intended. Therefore they hold regular progress review meetings to build accountability into their management routine. These reviews develop focus within the teams and keep the pressures of everyday work life from causing slippage.

These focused review meetings take place outside of regular staff meetings. Their frequency depends on the complexity of the initiative and its progress. With regular reviews, management can make simple corrections while maintaining the original schedule.

Regular review meetings allow management to keep teams accountable and to measure progress towards the desired results.

Example: Accountability

Paul understood that customer service was a key success factor in developing competitive advantage. He established a HPA to develop the best customer service for his market area but he was unsure how to effectively measure it. Paul knew that his customers expected to get all the job specifications identified and a schedule determined with one call. Simple concepts such as measuring the number of calls a service rep made would establish work criteria but would not effectively measure customer expectations. With thought Paul was able to identify metrics that his management system could generate that would give the information his customer service team needed to evaluate their progress in meeting their goal.

Accountability and the Leader

A CEO who exhibits strong leadership is best positioned to create accountability for results and outstanding performance. A CEO plays four key leadership roles:

1. Building a culture that values company objectives above individual ambition and in which everyone works toward the same objective.

2. Building a culture of trust. In this environment, team members understand that they can be vulnerable with each other without fear of personal attack and political retribution. They solve problems more quickly because they make decisions based on objective input from the outset.

Management teams with a high degree of trust are cohesive and function at a high level.

3. Avoid becoming the accountability taskmaster. Effective CEOs trust the team to do the work and hold each other accountable. Without trust, team members will hesitate to accept this role.

4. Personally setting the tone for absolute focus on results. When team members sense that the CEO lacks focus, they too will lack focus.

As we discussed in Chapter 10, CEOs of small and medium sized companies have an advantage over their larger brethren. Leadership in a smaller organization is less complex and results are easier to accomplish and simpler to measure.

Advantages of teamwork also accrue in smaller companies. In large companies managers may not have strong personal relationships. Large organizations also foster an advancement mentality through regular promotions. In smaller companies managers understand promotions are longer term. Consequently they focus on responsibility and personal development. They have longer relationships and know each other better so they may be more team oriented.

Much has been written about teamwork and the phrase is greatly overused. In practice effective teamwork is elusive. A good leader establishes a HPA for its development. He understands the difficulty of accomplishing effective teamwork and doesn't expect quick results. A simple to read in depth discussion of the leadership of accountability and teamwork can be found in *The Five Dysfunctions of a Team*, by Patrick Lencioni.

Summary

The success with which management holds itself and its teams accountable is the key to a company's future. Lack of accountability produces extreme frustration when it leads to lack of desired results.

Effective accountability is simple in concept but difficult to practice in that it requires good execution. Accountability is best accomplished when we:

- Have a solid foundation and work to a clear strategic plan.
- Have identified specific metrics.

- Hold regular progress reviews.

The role of the leader is extremely important.

The effective CEO builds a culture of trust within the management team and a culture of valuing the organization over the individual.

He builds a team that works openly without personal and political agendas.

Most importantly, the CEO acts as the organization's role model for effective accountability. He sets the standard for creating results by demonstrating an unwavering resolve to achieve initiatives. He follows the maxim "inspect what you expect" by reviewing progress and insisting that deadlines be met. He creates results by keeping himself accountable even as he provides accountability for his management and working teams.

___

Chapter 11 Best Ideas

Accountability requires good metrics.

Inspect what you expect.

Strong leadership is necessary for effective accountability.

My Best Ideas and Goals to Meet Them

_____

_____

_____

_____

_____

12
Building Excellence At All Levels

"All organizations are perfectly designed to get the results they are now getting. If we want different results, we must change the way we do things."
Anon

By now you will realize that minimizing the five hidden mistakes doesn't happen in a vacuum. It takes a coordinated process to move your company to the next level.

Figure One summarizes the five mistakes and links them together in what I call strategic development, an integrated model that is effective tactically and strategically.

Lack of focus is the most basic mistake because it is tactically and strategically important. Focus is both individual and organizational. When we focus ourselves, our team and our organization, we generate outstanding results.

Tactically we identify the key HPA tasks that are not urgent but important. Focus provides the ability to act on them and successfully achieve them. Strategically focus gets the management team on the same page and the right page. To paraphrase Drucker, we become very good at working on the right things.

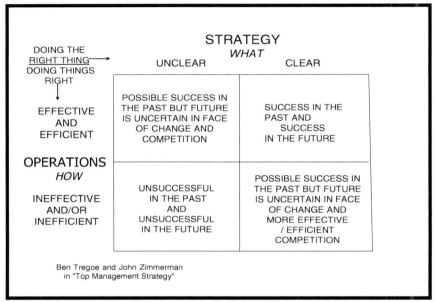

Figure One

Development and practice are primarily tactical. Improving the productivity and leadership of our key people can quickly generate improved results.

In Chapter 4 we discussed the difference between training and development. Development is specifically designed to change behaviors and attitudes. Development is results based. We specify a process and end up with predetermined results. Training improves efficiency, development improves effectiveness.

Here are examples of improvements we can realize from personal development:

- You are able to manage your overburdened work load for maximum results.
- Employees understand your vision and don't work at cross purposes.

- Your managers generate steady improvement in their departments.
- You spend less time as a referee of people issues.

Planning is primarily strategic. As we have discussed, a strategic plan provides definite competitive advantage leading to sustainable results.

Accountability is both tactical and strategic and is the key to realizing expected results in both areas.

Implementing Strategic Development

Figure Two shows what is required to build excellence in an organization.

Future Vision
- **Grow Revenue & Profits**
- **Beat the Competition**
- **Innovate & Lead**

Strategic Plan
A "must-have" road map for achieving leadership's Future Vision

Leadership Ability | **People Productivity**
Leadership, people support, and productivity necessary to implement Strategic Plan

Results-Based Culture
Enthusiastic, motivated, confident team of employees committed to achieving the organization's Future Vision

Figure Two

For effective strategic development there needs to be
- a clear definition of a desired future
- effective operations.

Both are critical to success. Over time, as the five mistakes are minimized, the organization will develop competitive advantage in its marketplace.

Strong leaders know that to realize their vision they must transform their company's operation at every level, from management and people productivity to planning processes and even the underlying culture.

The vision of the organization is a key part of the strategic planning process. CEOs should involve all key employees in defining the company's future vision.

Vision statements are often static and even trite. A good vision should be holistic to motivate employees and other stakeholders. A well crafted vision motivates employees not only financially but addresses their principles, values and beliefs.

Developing a motivating vision in non-profit organizations is relatively simple. People are attracted to the organization because they believe in the service. The challenge in a for-profit company is to craft a vision that fully motivates employees not just for financial gain but gives them the opportunity to serve the greater good.

The plan is the single most important activity a company's management team can undertake. The plan's purpose is to generate pre-determined, consistent results. It is a thorough, concise roadmap showing how the organization plans to achieve its vision.

The second component of strategic development, effective operations, can be broken into people productivity and leadership culture.

In Chapter 4 we discussed the difference between training and development. Training in specific skills is important for efficiency. Organizational productivity is a function of effective management and can be characterized by the degree to which individual employees and teams are effective and efficient on a daily basis. Managers' HPA drive the results of employees and teams.

Managers determine the organizational environment. The environment provides the culture and tools individual employees need to enhance skills, manage time, set goals, measure results and be more productive.

Leadership ability is the way in which employees are dealt with and communicated with daily. The effectiveness of leadership style directly impacts behaviors throughout the organization.

Strategic development is really about the growth of all the employees who make up the organization. Effective leadership is necessary and an ongoing catalyst for strategic development. Organizational development is people development. Effective CEOs understand that to control their destiny, they must continually evaluate their company's strategy and tactics at all levels.

All organizations have a present and a future. The strength of the processes used to run the business determines the quality of the future. To create a future different from the present, companies must strengthen processes. Change is accomplished through the actions of the employees.

It seems simple. Build a culture and team filled with enthusiastic, motivated, confident, committed employees who are accountable, empowered and committed to achieving their company's future vision.

Easy to say, difficult to do. Employees are the change agents. However, unless management creates a culture of change with strong leadership, continuous productivity improvement and effectiveness, the employees will not change and the company will not realize its vision of the future.

A Four Step Strategy to Implement Success
Stage 1: Awareness

Organizational culture provides the foundation for excellence. Successful CEOs build a culture where employees want to be and do their best, resulting in a high performance culture of enthusiastic, motivated, confident, committed people working as a team.

Effective leaders exhibit strong organizational awareness in that they understand their management structure, their predominant leadership style and the company culture. This includes understanding the nature of company controls, management flexibility, use of authority, motivational style and shared values.

These leaders also have strong self-awareness and a deep understanding of their strengths, emotions, limitations, values and motives. They are realistic and honest about themselves. They personally work to improve their management and leadership capabilities.

Organizational awareness sparks insight into the capacities and abilities that build organizational excellence.

Stage 2: Strategic Planning

Lack of focus in the management team is a key weakness of many organizations, resulting in managers who run off in all directions and even work at cross purposes. Successful strategic planning focuses the management team. Every one is on the same page and it's the right page. Focus drives performance, performance drives results.

The message is simple: strategic planning is fundamental to developing organizational focus. Effective strategy generates a significant competitive advantage in your marketplace.

Stage 3: People Development

Leaders must continually develop the effectiveness of key team members in order to achieve success. When key employees maintain a daily focus, they generate steady results.

Small changes in the effectiveness of key employees leverage into much larger improvements in profitability. People development becomes a competitive advantage.

Stage 4: Results Management

We put it all together by integrating an effective results management system within the other stages.

The purpose is to develop sustainable results from year to year by building goal setting, accountability and measurement into the daily fabric of the organization.

The best plans and development programs are only as good as their implementation. We must make a coordinated, consistent effort to ensure that daily urgent priorities do not take precedence over meeting our strategic goals.

Let's tie the five mistakes together with another example.

Case Study

Situation

Scott, the CEO of a transportation outsourcing company, was experiencing stagnation. The company was not growing, profitability was weak and people problems were sapping his energy. Scott had strong industry knowledge but was beginning to doubt his abilities as a leader and business owner.

Solution

The challenge Scott faced seemed simple enough to resolve: hire productive employees and increase revenue. He started by working with his management team to develop focus and clarity of direction. With a facilitator he conducted a four-day goal setting retreat. He used a development program to build effectiveness. In a short time communication noticeably improved on all levels and there was a renewed clarity of direction. Decisions that had previously taken hours to make were being resolved in a few minutes and with more effective results.

Scott then took the next step by working with his management team to plan the vision, purpose and mission for the company. They began by writing a vision statement showing where they pictured the company being in the next five years. They defined a goal to be a $50 million company in six years.

Outcome

The company is well on its way to achieving its goals. With a clear vision understood by all employees, the entire staff is working towards shared goals. Revenue growth is progressing according to plan. Gross profit margin increased 10% in two years. Net profit has tripled.

Scott is energized, "It feels good to be running the company, instead of the company running me."

What did Scott and his team do? They overcame the five hidden mistakes. They focused their talents, developed individually and as a team, practiced, planned and executed. The financial and personal ROIs were substantial and greatly exceeded the costs.

This is a key concept. The effective CEO doesn't view development and planning as a cost but as an investment. The CEO's challenge is to realize a positive return on this investment.

Summary

Effective CEOs accept the challenge to earn a positive return on their investment in planning and development. They understand they need to drive future performance to generate improved results and use proven methods to effect the change they envision.

Both clear strategy and effective operations are critical to organizational success. When we have neither we have not been successful in the past and most likely will not be so in the future.

When we are good operationally but have no strategy, we have possibly had success in the past but our future is uncertain in the face of change and competition. The same is true if we have had good strategy but ineffective operations.

The best place to start creating success is to develop and implement a strategic plan. Planning is strategically the single most important activity a management team can engage in. It is a thorough, concise roadmap to how an organization will move toward its future vision.

People make change. The ongoing transformation of an organization is the result of the growth of the people who make up the organization. Organizational development is in actuality people transformation.

Effective leadership is the ongoing catalyst that creates this strategic transformation.

Clear strategy and effective operations bring us to the optimal condition: we have had success in the past and will have more in the future. Organizations in this state increase revenue and profits year to year, outperform the competition, and innovate and lead in their marketplace. They have built excellence at all levels. They control their destiny.

Chapter 12 Best Ideas

Development and strategy are investments for the future.

Vision is key to committed employee involvement.

For sustained results there needs to be a clear definition of a desired future and effective operations

My Best Ideas and Goals to Meet Them

_____

_____

_____

_____

_____

_____

13
Leadership is Personal Action

**"We need to become the change
we want to see in our organization."
Gandhi**

You are successful right now. You may have more to accomplish but you are where you are because of your attitudes, ability and persistence.

Managing and leading an organization is difficult. People are difficult. They need attention. With your leadership, your organization has risen to its current level. With your continued leadership it will achieve your vision. Your leadership is instrumental to developing your organization's underlying culture – an enthusiastic, motivated, confident team of employees committed to achieving your future vision.

We all want personal and business success. It is your task to eliminate failure from your organization and help your employees with their success.

The single biggest reason that people fail in life is that they never take effective action. Indecision and fear are common obstacles to success. However, obstacles can be overcome when the individual makes a commitment to take action.

Successful people don't sit around waiting for everything to be "100 percent" right or to be "absolutely sure" they will succeed. They assess the opportunity and, if it has positive potential, they strike out boldly and energetically. They know life doesn't provide absolutes.

Successful people understand that the cost of failure is very modest compared to the cost of inaction. Failure means you are smarter the next time. Inaction means there is no next time, only a lifetime of unfulfilled opportunity.

In Chapter 12 we discussed the organizational requirements to attain competitive advantage and sustained results. In this chapter we will discuss effective leadership, building on the concepts outlined in Chapters 6 and 7.

Historical Perspective

The Second World War and Korean conflict were instrumental in shaping our management culture over the last 60 years. Our veterans were trained in the military command and control leadership style. This leadership approach had generated great success in war so it was natural for them to use this style as they moved into management in all of our organizations.

Many companies have been very successful using the command and control, type "A" management model. These managers are appreciated because when they are given a task they generate results. On the other hand, because they are task oriented, they often do not appreciate their employees and are hard to work for.

Over the years academic research has evaluated organizations to determine if performance differences could be identified. Research was conducted to determine the traits of highly successful leaders and tie these findings to organizational success. Collectively the research has determined there is a much more effective method than command and control to manage organizations and lead people. In previous chapters we have discussed several of the leading studies. Here is a brief summary tying them together. This is by no means complete; I only highlight conclusions over time.

In the 1960s Douglas McGregor, a management professor at the MIT Sloan School of Management, identified an approach to creating an environment within which employees are motivated by authority, direction and control or integration and self-control, which he called Theory X and Theory Y.

Theory X assumes that the average person:

- Dislikes work and attempts to avoid it.
- Has no ambition and wants no responsibility
- Is self-centered and does not care about organizational goals.
- Resists change.

Theory X assumes people work only for money and security.

Theory Y makes the following general assumptions:

- Work can be as natural as play and rest.
- People will be self-directed to meet their work objectives if they are committed to them.
- People will be committed to their objectives if rewards that address higher needs such as self-fulfillment are in place.
- Under these conditions, people will seek responsibility.

Theory Y assumes people work for their enjoyment and growth.

In the 1970's Jay Hall, PhD conducted a study to determine if the behavioral characteristics that the top achieving leaders employed set them apart from their lesser achieving colleagues. He started with over 60,000 managers and co-workers and eventually included over 100,000 interviews from across many industries. It is the largest controlled study ever completed.

Hall found definite commonalities among high achievers. He defined the various behavioral leadership traits and identified the "Developer" as the most successful. Developer leaders were most highly valued by their respective companies, were promoted faster and given the most responsibility for managing their organization's assets and people. Developer leaders have a theory Y philosophy. Hall's leadership types are discussed in Chapter 5.

Daniel Goleman, PhD added to the research in the 90's. We all know examples of people with high IQs who are not particularly successful. We intuitively understand there is not a strong correlation between Intellectual Intelligence, IQ, and business success. Goleman coined the phrase "Emotional Intelligence," EI, to distinguish the behavioral traits of a successful leader. Developer leaders are emotionally intelligent. See Chapter 3 and Appendix Three.

Jim Collins, author of *Good to Great*, in the first decade of this century added an organizational component to the research. He studied companies of equal capability and industry over a 20-year period to determine why one greatly excelled as compared to the other. He found that great companies are lead by "Level 5 leaders," individuals with a unique blend of personal humility and professional will. These leaders are servant leaders, not self-serving ones. They lead by asking questions, not giving answers; by dialog and debate, not coercion. They are Developer leaders.

The military is also changing. Captain Michael Abrashoff in his recent book *It's Your Ship* writes about the tremendous positive changes generated when he changed from command and control to a developer leadership style.

Patrick Lencioni, author of *The Five Dysfunctions of a Team*, carries the Developer style to effective teamwork. Much has been written about teamwork yet attaining it is still an elusive goal for many organizations. Lencioni describes how to develop trust and accountability in teams. His successful teams have a theory Y philosophy, are EI savvy and have Developer leaders.

The results Developer leaders create are astonishing. Top achievers exhibit consistent behavioral characteristics. Most impressively these leaders use these characteristics to create an environment of involvement, commitment, and creativity that propels their teams to great heights of achievement.

Significantly, the work of Hall, Goleman and others validates the idea that these traits can be learned. Managers and leaders can improve their effectiveness.

Personal Leadership

You are a role model. Everything counts. Your employees observe you and your traits. John Maxwell is fond of saying, "People do what people see."

Your personal leadership is a reflection of you and your expectations for you and your organization. Many components make up personal leadership, the most basic being leading a balanced life, having a positive mental attitude, building relationships built on trust and regularly improving your effectiveness at managing and leading.

Effective leadership starts with a realistic awareness of your personal strengths and weaknesses. Effective CEOs clearly understand themselves and the people in their organization. They build strong interpersonal effectiveness into their organizations, creating an environment where everyone works together with trust and openness.

Organizations built on competitiveness between departments and in the marketplace do not easily establish trust. People may be difficult and hard to understand. Many leaders have a poorly developed ability to read others.

This is why effective CEOs use surveys to assess personality characteristics that correlate highly with job success. These surveys provide strategic intelligence that shows why people behave the way they do. Good assessments have a high degree of accuracy and meet legal guidelines.

Basic assessments are limited to evaluating a few traits such as introversion/extroversion and dominance/submissiveness. Higher order assessments may measure up to ten traits and correlate them closely with job success.

Assessments have three uses:

1. At their most basic, assessments describe individual characteristics. They are commonly used in hiring, helping to avoid the problem of hiring someone only to find out they don't meet expectations. Surveys help determine whether a person will be a team player in a given culture before they are hired. Numerous studies show that using assessments reduces hiring mistakes and turnover by up to 30%.

2. Assessments may also be diagnostic and predictive. They tell us why a manager is the way she is. Once we know why, we can predict how she will behave in new situations. We minimize promotion mistakes that cause organizational problems and distract from productive work.

3. High order surveys are developmental. They provide the foundation needed for executives to coach employees to a higher level of success. These surveys address leadership, communication and productivity. They define personal

characteristics so management can help individuals achieve personal dynamic balance and interpersonal team balance.

Example: Use of Surveys

Scott, the CEO of the transportation company discussed in Chapter 12, was experiencing difficulties hiring the right people. Sales were stagnant and turnover was high. Through an alliance, Scott found an assessment that was instrumental in changing his people dynamics. First he used it to determine employee strengths and the right organizational fit. With this knowledge Scott divided sales responsibilities into two groups: account managers who maintain the business, and consultants who bring in new business. He restructured the sales staff from salary based positions to commission plans.

Using the assessment as part of his hiring process, Scott hired new employees who were dedicated and committed, with strengths that made positive contributions to the company. He used the assessment to determine the right fit for existing employees.

The results have been dramatic. Improving the hiring process by using the assessment has saved the company approximately one million dollars over the last four years. Recently the company made a profit on every single shipment in a one-month period as a result of having the right person managing the customer service department.

You run a multi-million dollar organization. Do you have balance in your personal life? How do you create and maintain balance? Are your key employees balanced? There is not much we have control over. Our personal balance is one area where we do have total control. Build balance in your life. Help your employees build their balance.

Leading requires a great deal of physical and emotional energy and can be draining. You have to persuade and say "let's go" to people who don't want to go. You make tough calls that directly affect the lives of other people. You have to solve difficult problems. You have to serve as a mediator, encourager and teacher to your team.

For this we need balance so we can re-energize ourselves. Reading, cooking, and sports are examples of how we can build balance in our lives. Develop methods that are interesting and enjoyable for you.

Balance is all about making the right choices. We all have to make hundreds of choices every day. It starts first thing in the morning. Do you eat a healthy breakfast or do you eat a sugar laden muffin with a specialty Starbucks loaded with whipped cream?

As the day goes along, our decisions generally get more complicated and difficult to make. In our position, choices don't come accompanied by the facts necessary for a simple conclusion.

Right choices begin with an accepting self-image. Be realistic in acknowledging who you are and where you stand now. Have a healthy self-respect. With that kind of self-image you are not wholly controlled by the need to win the approval of others.

Know what you stand for. Be aware of your values. Be confident that they are ethically sound and bring out the best in you and your team. People respect a leader with strong values and will enthusiastically follow his lead.

When you have a positive self-image and strong values, you don't have to make compromises to please others. Your choices, even when difficult, will be understood and respected by your team.

Positive mental attitude is one of the three traits we discussed in Chapter 6. Attitude can make or break us individually and organizationally. We have a choice, every day, regarding the attitudes we embrace. Do you frequently complain or are you positive and always looking for solutions? A positive attitude does not magically happen. It needs to be cultivated and strengthened.

Executives with leadership responsibility face stress and strain every day. For us a positive attitude is a tough attitude. Toughness makes it possible for you to resist great strain without coming apart.

Circumstances outside our control impose stress on us. A tough mental attitude keeps us from losing heart. We do not fall into doubt or give up in despair. We hang on, endure the knocks, and come out stronger than before.

Your attitude defines you. Others notice and respond accordingly.

Successful CEOs don't try to do it all by themselves. They develop mastermind alliances with others who have the expertise they need to develop organizational excellence important to the results and success they desire.

We will seek relationships when we have two attitudes:
- that knowledge is key to future improvement
- that we want to learn how to manage and lead more effectively.

Some potential alliances include:

1. Technical Requirements

Many executives regularly confer with others who have technical expertise beyond what is internal to the company. This can take several forms; a technical board of advisors, an industry group or simply personal relationships with outside experts.

2. Functional Areas

A typical example is sales. Companies often reach a plateau when the sales department grows to the point where employees and processes would benefit from experience not available in house. Successful CEOs seek expert advice.

3. People Development

Most companies have maintenance budgets; IT for example. We all say people are our most important asset. Often the largest overhead expense is the combined salary of our management team from first level supervision through senior management. How many have a budget to improve the effectiveness of their key people? Personnel development is specifically designed to improve effectiveness by changing behaviors and attitudes. A small improvement in the effectiveness of key people has a great impact on the bottom line.

4. Strategic Planning

Organizations with a specific plan significantly out-perform other companies of equal capability by having up to 45% higher revenue per employee. The message is simple: planning develops focus; focus drives performance; performance drives results. Planning gives us a strong competitive advantage in the marketplace.

Building alliances with outside experts is easy to understand. Building alliances inside the organization is easy as well. Give your employees the opportunity to expand and grow. Give them an opportunity and let them surprise you with their results.

None of these suggestions will be effective unless we regularly improve our capability to manage and lead by maintaining a program of personal transformation.

In Chapter 6 we discussed the long term importance of the 1% solution to our personal careers. We can steadily improve, allowing us to develop personal expertise and sustainable results personally and organizationally. We accomplish this through using HPA to focus on those tasks and traits important to our success. Use the process outlined in Chapter 8 to build your success. Success breeds more success. As we build effectiveness we build a positive attitude.

Organizational Leadership

Equally important is our ability to lead others. Effective leaders understand that their success is dependent on the success of their employees. People follow the leader not for what they can do for him but for what he can do for them. The Developer leader understands this and builds a high performance culture by working through people. The most important leadership traits are building a vision that engages all your people, sharing power and leading with a servant's heart.

The vision you and your management team develop must be inspirational and motivational and be based on your employees' principles, values and beliefs. The vision establishes the foundation for the future of the organization. The more employees relate to it the more effective the organization will become.

Sharing power is one of the most important traits a Developer leader can have. Your key managers want to contribute to the direction and initiatives of the organization. Sharing power with them is an effective method of planning, developing best thinking, creating positive change and a molding a culture where people want to work.

The result of sharing power is organizational excellence. The company builds a competitive advantage in the marketplace by being proactive and leading rather than by being reactive and following.

In Chapter 5 we discussed servant leadership. Our employees work for themselves, follow the leader for what he can do for them and want to feel appreciated.

A sophisticated view is that you are paying your employees to work for themselves. In reality we all work for ourselves.

The Emotional Intelligence Social Competencies in Appendix Three are the foundation of servant leadership. Many managers can make significant improvements in these traits. Empathy is the most important. Developing a service mentality and developing others are also important.

Summary

There is much we can't control but we do control our attitude, our learning and our development. Attitude is important. The only difference between winners and losers is that losers quit.

Losers procrastinate because of their fear of taking risks. A very good way to overcome the fear of risk taking is to set clear, written, measurable goals, and then review them regularly.

Focus personally and organizationally. Return to Chapter 8 and write the behaviors you want to strengthen. Set measurable goals to improve. Get the action steps into your schedule. Hold yourself accountable and watch yourself change. Observe the positive reaction others have to your changes. Take great pride in the changes you make and that you bring to the organization.

Make continual learning a priority. Develop the attitude that development and strategy are investments worthy of your commitment. Strive to be great. With these attitudes you won't become complacent. Complacency leads to lost momentum. Lost momentum leads to lower expectations and results. In this politically correct era, an analogy from sports says that we don't run up the score on a hapless competitor. No, do run up the score! Don't inhibit your momentum in building sustainable growth!

We are role models. Our employees look up to our leadership. When we are effective we have a high level of control over the learning and development of our team.

All of us aspire to reach our dreams and goals. The leader with a "Servant's Heart" inspires others who realize that he cares about them and wants them to succeed on a personal level. When people realize that they can reach their personal goals through helping the organization reach its goals, impressive results happen.

Servant Leadership at its most effective builds a culture of enthusiastic, motivated, and confident employees committed to achieving the company's future vision. Easy to say but hard to do. People work harder and more effectively in direct proportion to how much they respect and trust their leaders. Build your effectiveness in each area. Build your credibility. It's the foundation of effective leadership.

The caveat is that we never lessen our accountability for results. Jim Collins's level 5 leader demonstrates an unwavering resolve to do whatever must be done to produce the best long-term results. [4]

Successful leaders insist on a continuous process of planning and development, of accountability and results, and build the culture of the organization around these cornerstones.

Goal setting and leading with a Servants Heart are the two cornerstones for effective leadership. Both are necessary for a great organization.

As you meet your personal goals, you will revel in your success and confidence. To re-quote Scott, "It feels good to be running the company, instead of the company running me."

You are successful and comfortable as a leader at your present level. What personal HPA are you going to develop to take your leadership capabilities to a higher, more effective level?

---

[4] *Good To Great*, Jim Collins, Harper Collins, 2001, page 36

Chapter 13 Best Ideas

Leadership is personal

Attitude is important

Development and strategy are investments, not costs

My Best Ideas and Goals to Meet Them

_____

_____

_____

_____

_____

_____

_____

14
Blueprint for
Organizational Success

**"Even if you are on the right track,
but just sit there, you will still get run over"
Will Rogers**

You have learned many new concepts while reading this book. Because this wealth of information is so extensive, you might find it difficult to develop a plan to build an excellent organization.

The five mistakes are discussed in Chapters 1 through 11. In Chapter 12 we discussed strategic development as a model for building excellence in your organization. Chapter 13 discusses personalized leadership with suggestions on how to become an effective leader. This chapter distills all this information into a simple blueprint that will help you implement these concepts.

The key to any plan is to get started. Successful people don't wait. Once they have a vision, they start immediately even if they don't have all the information they need. They realize their clarity will continue to increase as they proceed.

You cannot transform your organization without understanding. In Chapter 13 we talked about the value of developing personal awareness. Development of organizational awareness is of equal importance. When you use assessments, you gain a high degree of awareness of the knowledge foundation your company currently has. Gaining knowledge will improve all areas of business including hiring, communication, structure, culture and leadership.

In our discussion of strategic development, we determined that there are three major components to organizational excellence: clear strategy, effective leadership and people productivity. See Figure One below. These do not stand alone. They work together to create a strong synergy. Weakness in any one drains the power of the other two and significantly reduces organizational capability. For example, if the leadership culture is poor even though strategy and productivity are relatively high, the company culture will be poor and the organization will under perform.

Figure One

A good survey will measure whether employees perceive the organizational structure as bureaucratic or versatile, the leadership style as directive or participative and the organizational culture as competitive or supportive. It will determine how large a gap exists between employee perceptions of their actual situation vs. their ideal situation. It allows management to see the differences between employee groups. An example of such useful knowledge is the gap between management and employee perceptions.

Where you start your transformation - developing clear strategy, productivity or leadership culture - depends on your organizational awareness and financial, market and other conditions. With informed knowledge you will be able to start where you will get the strongest improvement and highest ROI.

Your internal assessment of your capability in the three areas, your experience in driving change, the time you have available to lead the effort and the political and cultural considerations involved will help you determine whether you can complete the process in house or whether you need to build an alliance with outside experts.

Starting with development is one option. Small changes in effectiveness can bring large changes in the bottom line. A sound development program can provide as much as a 10 to 1 return on your investment.

Many confuse seminars with development. Changing behaviors and attitudes is a long term process. Seminars produce only a feel good result. Yes, they impart good knowledge and participants become enthused, but it is up to them to incorporate what they have learned to into their everyday routine. Most people don't. They have good intentions but after a short time they return to the status quo.

If you are inexperienced at using a development process, take a measured approach. Don't make a large, expensive investment that is outside your comfort zone until you have gained the experience and knowledge that is required to achieve high returns.

Start with one manager or team from one department where you feel change can bring quick and positive returns. Identify the results you want to achieve and set those as the standard for the program. Work at the behavioral and attitudinal level, the way we act and think, to ensure long lasting change. Set clear metrics to measure your success and return on investment.

Development takes your focus. You have to exhibit ownership and emphasis for best results.

Alternatively you may start by developing a clear strategy. In Chapter 9 we showed how strategic planning provides tremendous competitive advantage. Strategic focus is the cornerstone of an outstanding organization.

A good plan must combine strong analysis with considered thought, a process that can take significant time. Don't try to short circuit this phase because it is the foundation for all that follows.

Be wary of third parties who offer to help with the analysis. You and your management team have experience and insight into your business. Use it. Develop ownership of the plan by your executive team. Direct customer contact and subsequent analysis is a very effective way to achieve their strong commitment.

Strategic planning is one area where you should seriously consider building outside alliances. How many of you have ever read a book on strategic planning or lead a planning session in an organized manner? Many companies are able to conduct team functions internally but some situations, such as high level strategic planning and setting objectives for the future, are too important to complete at less than the highest level.

A skilled facilitator has the experience to bring out the best from all participants. As a neutral party, they are outside the corporate politics and hierarchical structures that limit your effectiveness when you lead the process. In a neutral environment, they help fragile thoughts blossom to great concepts. Their systems are proven, ensuring that the organization's plan is the product of the team's best input and that the team has complete buy-in.

Remember, the plan is only the first step of a three-phase process. Distill the plan into operating objectives for the next year. Develop metrics to measure progress.

A plan without execution won't bring the expected results. The results management phase is very important. If you don't make a concentrated and continuous effort to manage this process, the daily need to generate revenue will take precedence.

As with development, your leadership and commitment from the analysis to the results management phase is key to the success of the planning process.

Summary

The steps for your blueprint are straightforward. They are easy to understand but difficult to implement. Successful transformation to an outstanding organization takes your focused and continuous commitment.

Follow this blueprint for success.

- Develop a knowledge foundation with organizational awareness.
- Get started with either development or strategy.
- Remember that changing behaviors and attitudes is a long term process.
- Measure your progress to identify your ROI.
- Prepare an annual development plan.
- Annually review your strategic plan.
- Provide continuous leadership.

The five mistakes are simply business blocking and tackling. They are basic to building an outstanding company and unleashing your potential. We all do them to some extent. Improve their execution and reap the rewards. As you overcome the five hidden mistakes you and your company will:

- Raise effectiveness to the highest level
- Improve the your competitive advantage
- Generate sustainable results in revenue and profitability
- Develop innovation in your marketplace

You have to make a conscious focused effort to overcome the status quo. You must lead the process both for yourself and your organization. When you do your personal benefits are substantial:

- Running your organization rather than it running you
- Earning professional and personal admiration
- Waking in the morning thinking about opportunity and success
- Becoming more significant in the lives of others
- Achieving your personal vision

Would you rather face pain on a daily basis or generate long term excellence? Start now to create your organization's foundation for success.

Chapter 14 Best Ideas

Organizational awareness is the foundation of informed knowledge.

Start with a program you are comfortable with.

Regularly review progress.

My Best Ideas and Goals to Meet Them

_____

_____

_____

_____

_____

_____

_____

Appendix One

About the Author

As the former CEO and principal of three successful businesses, **Tom Northup** understands the complexities faced by today's busy executives. He is experienced in high growth situations, new product start-ups, strategic planning, market analysis, teamwork, and turn-arounds.

Today, through coaching, consulting, mentoring, and training, Tom provides practical experience and thoughtful leadership. He is a goal-oriented executive experienced in developing strong management teams all with a focus on building sustainable success and results.

He works side-by-side with clients to develop plans and implement strategies to . . .

- build capabilities that increase revenue and profitability year after year

- heighten competitive advantages

- make companies more proactive in the marketplace

- build effective management teams

- foster greater corporate wide accountability

- generate sustained results

- groom future generations of leaders

- ensure continuity of vision and growth through thoughtful succession planning

Tom has CEO Experience. He personally understands how to build excellence and reach a vision for the future.

Tom is results oriented. He helps clients meet hard-to-reach objectives.

Tom's process is transformational. He helps make behavioral and attitudinal changes for long-lasting success.

Tom is practical. He provides proven methods and practical how-tos.

Tom is affiliated with Leadership Management Institute (LMI), of Waco, Texas. Established in 1966, LMI is an international training and development company with more than 40 years of experience helping individuals and organizations develop and use more of their true potential.

Tom can be reached by phone at 949-553-9634 or by email at Tomn@LMGsuccess.com

His website is www.LMGsuccess.com.

Appendix Two

Questions to Frame
High Payoff Activities

1. How can I create and communicate a clear vision for the part of the business that I manage?
2. What can I do to think more strategically every day?
3. How can I provide clear performance objectives to the people with whom I work?
4. How can I encourage my employees to add value?
5. How can I create an atmosphere in which people feel included and valued?
6. How can I help my people succeed?
7. How can I communicate better?
8. What can I do to be a better leader?
9. What can I do to maximize the talents of those who work for me?
10. What can I do to make sure that people have the knowledge and tools they need to be successful?
11. How can I create a meaningful set of metrics to measure our work?
12. How can I create systems to make our work more error free?
13. How can I build better relationships with our customers, with our suppliers?
14. How can I increase the value our customers receive?
15. What tasks can I delegate that will allow me to work on important issues and will help develop the person I delegate to?
16. How can I evaluate people more effectively?

Appendix Three[5]

Emotional Intelligence Domains and Competencies

Personal Competence: How we manage ourselves.
SELF-AWARENESS
- *Emotional self-awareness:* Reading one's own emotions and recognizing their impact; using gut sense to guide decisions
- *Accurate self-assessment:* Knowing one's strengths and limits
- *Self-confidence:* A sound sense of one's self-worth and capabilities

SELF-MANAGEMENT
- *Emotional self-control:* Keeping disruptive emotions and impulses under control
- *Transparency:* Displaying honesty and integrity; trustworthiness
- *Adaptability:* Flexibility in adapting to changing situations or overcoming obstacles
- *Achievement:* The drive to improve performance to meet inner standards of excellence
- *Initiative:* Readiness to act and seize opportunities
- *Optimism:* Seeing the upside in events

Social Competence: How we manage relationships
SOCIAL AWARENESS
- *Empathy:* Sensing others' emotions, understanding their perspective, and taking active interest in their concerns
- *Organizational awareness:* Reading the currents, decision networks, and politics at the organizational level

---

[5] Pg. 39. *Primal Leadership, Realizing The Power Of Emotional Intelligence*, Daniel Goleman, Richard Boyatzis, Annie McKee, Harvard Business School Press, 2002

- *Service:* Recognizing and meeting follower, client or customer needs

RELATIONSHIP MANAGEMENT

- *Inspirational leadership:* Guiding and motivation with a compelling vision
- *Influence:* Wielding a range of tactics for persuasion
- *Developing others:* Bolstering others' abilities through feedback and guidance
- *Change catalyst:* Initiating, managing and leading in a new direction
- *Conflict management:* Resolving disagreements
- *Teamwork and collaboration:* Cooperation and team building

Appendix Four[6]

Interpersonal Behavior Flaws Performed By One Person Against Another

Check yourself against this list. Pick one or two and use the self directed learning in Chapter 8 to change your behavior. Successful people don't exhibit too many of these traits so don't be too hard on yourself.

1. Winning too much: The need to win at all costs and in all situations – when it matters and when it doesn't.
2. Adding too much value: The overwhelming desire to add our two cents to every discussion.
3. Passing judgment: The need to rate others and impose our standards on them.
4. Making destructive comments: The needless sarcasms and cutting remarks that we think make us sound sharp and witty.
5. Starting with "No," "But" or "However:" The overuse of these negative qualifiers secretly says, "I'm right, you're wrong."
6. Telling the world how smart we are: The need to show people we're smarter than they think we are.
7. Speaking when angry: Using emotional volatility as a management tool.
8. Negativity, or "Let me explain why that won't work:" The need to share our negative thoughts even when we weren't asked.

---

[6] Pg. 40, 41 *What Got You Here Won't Get You There*, Marshall Goldsmith, Hyperion 2007

9. Withholding information: The refusal to share information in order to maintain an advantage over others.
10. Failing to give proper recognition: The inability to praise and reward.
11. Claiming credit that we don't deserve: The most annoying way to overestimate our contribution to any success.
12. Making excuses: The need to reposition our annoying behavior as a permanent fixture so people excuse us for it.
13. Clinging to the past: The need to deflect blame away from ourselves and onto events and people from our past.
14. Playing favorites: Failing to see that we are treating someone unfairly.
15. Refusing to express regret: The inability to take responsibility for our actions, admit we're wrong, or recognize how our actions affect others.
16. Not listening: The most passive-aggressive form of disrespect for colleagues.
17. Failing to express gratitude: The most basic form of bad manners.
18. Punishing the messenger: The misguided need to attack the innocent who are usually only trying to help us.
19. Passing the buck: The need to blame everyone but ourselves.
20. An excessive need to be "me:" Exalting our faults as virtues simply because they're who we are.

Bibliography

This is not a complete list of references. It is current material that is easy to read and books I use in my practice.

Abrashoff, Captain Michael D. 2002. *It's Your Ship*, New York: Warner Business Books

Below, Patrick, Morrisey, George L. and Acomb, Betty L. 1987. *The Executive Guide To Strategic Planning*, San Francisco: Jossey-Bass 20 years old, still in print.

Bossidy, Larry and Charan, Ram. 2002. *Execution; The Discipline of Getting Things Done*, New York: Crown Books
Big company discussion; the principles and focus are valuable lessons.

Devries, Henry J. and Stiehl, Chris. 2008. *Pain Killer Marketing: How to Turn Customer Pain into Market Gain*, El Monte: Wbusiness Books

Canfield, Jack. 2005. *The Success Principles*, New York: HarperCollins

Collins, Jim. 2001. *Good To Great*, New York: HarperCollins

Goleman, Daniel, Boyatzis, Richard and McKee, Annie. 2002. *Primal Leadership: Realizing The Power of Emotional Intelligence*, Boston: Harvard Business School Press
Goleman has written several books on EI. This is a good place to start.

Goldsmith, Marshall. 2007. *What Got You Here Won't Get You There*, New York: Hyperion

Hill, Andrew with Wooden, John. 2001. *Be Quick – But Don't Hurry*, New York: Simon and Schuster
John Wooden's success formula. Entertaining.

Kim, Chan W and Maubourgne, Renee. 2005. *Blue Ocean Strategy* Boston: Harvard Business School Press

Kosner, James M. and Posner, Barry Z. 2007. *The Leadership Challenge*, 4th Edition, San Francisco: Josey-Bass.

Lencioni, Patrick, 2002 *The Five Dysfunctions of a Team* San Francisco: Jossey-Bass
Lencioni has a companion work book.

Maxwell, John. 2007. *The 21 Irrefutable Laws of Leadership: Follow Them and People Will Follow You* Nashville: Thomas Nelson
Newly updated version of Maxwell's classic

Plotkin, Harris. 1997. *Building a Winning Team*, Glendale: Griffin Publishing
Plotkin discusses how to hire and the value of assessments.

Seligman, Martin E. 2006. *Learned Optimism: How to Change Your Mind And Your Life*, New York: Vintage
You determine how optimistic you are and learn how to develop a hopeful, healthy outlook.

Tregoe, Benjamin B. and Zimmerman, John W. 1980. *Top Management Strategy*, New York: Simon and Schuster

Index